BLOOD ON THE ESMERALDA

Michael Woodward *(standing)* with Patricio Guarda
and the Belgian sisters on an excursion, 1970

BLOOD ON THE ESMERALDA

The Life and Death of Father Michael Woodward

by

EDWARD CROUZET

DOWNSIDE

2002

CONTENTS

© 2002 Edward Crouzet

All rights reserved. No part of this book may be reproduced,
stored in a retrieval system or transmitted in any form or by any
means without the permission of the author. Printed and bound by
Hobbs the Printers, Totton, Hampshire SO40 3WX and published
by Downside Books, Stratton-on-the-Fosse, Radstock, BA3 4RH.

ISBN 1 898663 14 9

INTRODUCTION

In 1974, back in England after a time of living and working on a monastic mission in the jungle of southern Peru, I read a horrific article in the *Observer* about the torture and death of Michael Woodward on a prison ship in Valparaiso, Chile, as a consequence of the Pinochet coup.

I still missed Latin America and longed to return there if only for a visit. The *Observer* article not only fanned these feelings but also aroused some sense of identification. Like me, Michael Woodward had been a pupil at Downside School. He was five years older, but I remembered him clearly. He was the tallest boy in the School, was a prefect and took his turn at supervising the large prep room in which we small boys sat for hours every weekday evening. The demeanour and mannerisms of the prefect in charge were among the few distractions from the tedium of the prep. Their mettle was put to the test by various devices, but that is another story. The common School was not the only affinity I felt with the murdered priest. There had been elements of risk in Peru also: violence by rival traders against me because I helped local farmers to market their produce independently, hatred by embittered Marxist or Maoist intellectuals of gringo involvement with their country's poor, dangers from the mountain roads, the river and the jungle. In 1974 I knew nothing of the story leading up to Michael Woodward's death but I felt a certain identification with it. So I resolved in my own mind that one day, if and when the opportunity arose, I would travel to Chile and find out what I could of it.

It would have been difficult to investigate Michael's story during the dictatorship of Pinochet. By 1989, when this came to an end, I was Catholic Chaplain to the University of Bristol and had the time and money (a leaving present given by parents when I ceased being a housemaster at Downside School, for which I now thank them again) to visit Chile the following year. By this time I had been in contact with Michael's family in Spain and England.

The story was pieced together over three visits. But almost as soon as I started, my motivation changed: I became passionately involved in the search. Among the people I interviewed, some regarded Michael as naïve, some as humorous and eccentric, but all who had known him made clear their conviction that he was utterly straightforward, a man of integrity and deeply lived spirituality. By contrast the military authorities had spread the lie that he took advantage of his priesthood to indulge in irresponsible sexual behaviour. What was worse, distant family relatives who remained in Chile, and their social circles, believed this lie. My task became that of revealing his innocence, of exposing the injustice of which he was the victim and, by the same token, of telling a story which, though he will never be a canonized saint, will, I hope, shed a small light on ways in which the Church relates to the world, especially the world of the poor.

The book was largely written by those I met and interviewed and who made my task so wonderfully enriching an experience. They are acknowledged by name in the footnotes. There are others, not so acknowledged, whom I must thank for generously giving me free hospitality and accommodation, as well as informative discussion. They include Antonio and Monica Oneto in Vina del Mar, Maruja Celedon in Cerro Placeres, Valparaiso, the Jesuit students in Almirante Barroso, Santiago, Fr Patricio Carriola SJ, former Rector of the University of Antofagasta and, finally, my original contact in Chile, Fr Jose Aldunate SJ, Stonyhurst educated, now in his mid-eighties and almost blind, whose continuing and tireless work for human rights has to me been an inspiration.

Edward Crouzet O.S.B.
Bungay, 26th June 2001

CHAPTER ONE

BACKGROUND (1932-1954)

Michael Woodward was descended on his father's side from a wealthy Irish racehorse breeder whose daughter, the heir to his fortune, married a British Army officer, a Captain Woodward. They had one son, Edward Gerard Woodward, known as Roy, who was sent away at the age of five to board at King's School, Canterbury. Though originally destined for the Army like his father, when the time came, post-World War I cuts in recruitment denied him a place, so he joined the British American Tobacco Company instead. After brief postings in Denmark and the Argentine, in 1927 he was sent to Chile where he was to remain for the next twenty years, becoming Assistant Managing Director of BAT in that country.

Michael's maternal grandmother was also of Irish stock but brought up in Chile. She married Federico Yriberry, a businessman of Basque origins working in Valparaiso, who died in 1941. They had several children of whom one was Michael's mother, Mary, and lived in a large house near the railway station in Vina del Mar, the fashionable seaside resort and residential suburb to the north of the port city of Valparaiso. This house was to be Michael's surviving family base in Chile after his parents left the country in 1947 until his grandmother's death in 1962.

Roy Woodward married Mary Yriberry on the 12th April 1931. Mary had grown up a devout Catholic and Roy, who had been brought up in the Church of England, himself became a Catholic before the wedding. He remained faithful to the practice of his new religion right up to his death at an advanced age in 1999. Michael, their eldest child was born on 25th January 1932. Two years later they had twins, John and Jocelyn.

1

A second girl, Patricia, was born in 1938 and a third son, Peter, in 1942.

To a Chilean contemporary and friend of Michael's, Roy fitted the stereotype of the English gentleman: courteous, reserved and unimaginative. From his middle-class English education he had indeed acquired a habit of modesty and good manners which prevented him from speaking about himself, his feelings or his state of health. He had received no further education after leaving school and picked up his expert knowledge of the tobacco industry entirely from direct experience in factory and office. His imaginative powers, which Michael's friend failed to recognize, were channelled into practical projects such as the construction of the new family home in Vina del Mar: instead of the more usual bricks and cement this had mud and stud walls reinforced with wire mesh as a precaution against earthquakes. Inside it was lined with plywood panelling, curved at the corners, which gave it a modernist appearance while also being a practical solution to covering a mud wall. Roy's interest in the surrounding garden was more conventional: he vied with friends for the finest roses and the best croquet lawn. In their turn the children were encouraged to be practical. Each of them was given a patch of ground to cultivate and an instructor was brought in from BAT to teach them carpentry.[1]

If Roy was at home there were family outings and picnics. On ordinary days, however, when their father was working and Mary was taken up with the younger children, the older ones spent much of their time in the company of the servants with whom they spoke Spanish, though the family conversed among themselves in English. They all came together in the evening for dinner. The meal was kept under strict control by Roy. Everything on the children's plates had to be eaten up. If the conversation started to move in a direction Roy did not like, he uttered the word 'Sollocks', a term borrowed from the contemporary writer, Dornford Yates, to indicate his disapproval and put a stop to it.

Such forms of family discipline were fairly typical of that time and milieu, but it would not be surprising if later on the children reacted against it, consciously or unconsciously. Perhaps it is a coincidence, but none of the Woodward family chose to follow their father into business. In Michael's case, at least, this was a conscious decision. Later, when he was studying at the Seminary, he expressed the opinion that his father was 'immature', doubtless the view of the ardent novice who was convinced that he himself now knew what life was about. When Michael visited the family as a priest in later years, Roy was enraged by his sermons and disagreed strongly with his ideas. The relationship between father and eldest son had its affectionate and humorous side, but there was also a tension which eventually developed into mutual intolerance. If ideas came to be diametrically opposed, however, their manner of upholding and expressing them bore a certain resemblance.

Roy's strict control over the family was compensated by openness elsewhere. The servants, for example, had instructions to give food to any beggars who called at the house. Roy was popular with the employees of British American Tobacco. As the manager responsible for building the factories and running the manufacturing operations, he saw to it that not only housing, but proper medical and recreational facilities were provided for the workforce. The factory had its own crèche for the young mothers who worked there. Such attention to workers' needs has now long been a legal obligation in Chile, as elsewhere, and even at the time was doubtless good for morale and productivity, but care for workers' welfare was far from universal. Roy involved himself personally in their social events, joining in *fiestas* and dancing the

3

cueca, the typical Chilean country dance, with agricultural workers from the tobacco plantations owned by the Company. It was an effort for him to speak Spanish, but when there was a talk or speech to be given, his children would hear him practising the words for hours on end. Years later, with the sophistication of his Marxist viewpoint, Michael chose to see all this as patronising and exploitative, but at the time, when he was a young boy, it probably left its mark on his imagination.

Michael's Chilean contemporary who saw Roy as a 'typical English gentleman' was struck by what he called Mary's 'spirituality'.[2] Under her influence, with the support of her convert husband, the family was given a devout upbringing in the Catholic faith. Each evening, when they were small, Mary said night prayers with the children. They attended Mass as a family on Sundays, holidays of obligation and at other special times such as Holy Week. It was from his mother that Michael acquired his first religious inclinations.

Mary was imaginative: she enjoyed telling stories and sharing jokes with her children. She introduced them to classical music. Listening with them to recordings of Kreisler playing the violin concertos of Brahms and Mendelssohn, she would encourage them to 'feel the music sending shivers down your spine'. Michael was his mother's favourite child. During their summer holidays in the country, when much time was spent riding on horseback, it was Michael who cycled with his mother to the market. At other times he was sent out to do the shopping on his own. This closeness of the eldest son to his mother and a tendency on his part to order his younger brothers and sisters around for their own good earned him the nickname 'Bishop'. It was good-humoured: he never minded being teased and may even have invented the title himself. His sister Jocelyn, however, thought him 'a typical elder brother, insufferably bossy' and, when she was angry with him for lecturing her charge, the Chilean maid who looked after Pat would call him *Tayta,* meaning a sort of dictator. But Pat adored her eldest brother. The servants may have missed Michael's humour which showed itself at an early stage and stayed with him all his life.

For his first schooling Michael went to "Miss Hislop's", a small Dame school for English-speaking children in Vina. In 1941, at the age of 9, he was sent away as a boarder to the Grange School in Santiago. This was a British-style Prep and Public School combined. It prepared boys for the Common Entrance exam which admitted them either to the senior section of the Grange School itself or, in normal times, to a Public School in the United Kingdom. Crossing the Atlantic during the Second World War, however, would have been an unnecessary risk, so there was no question of boys leaving for England for a few years. The Headmaster, an Englishman named John Jackson, was a friend of the Woodward family.

Most of the Grange pupils were from well-to-do Chilean families and were sent there for the English Public School education as well, no doubt, as for the advantages which fluency in the English language would offer them later. It was a strict rule at the School that only English was to be spoken by the boys, even if they were Chilean. Anyone caught speaking Spanish was sent to the Headmaster to receive six strokes with the cane, a procedure which concluded with a gentlemanly handshake to show that there were no hard feelings on either side. Michael himself was able to thrive under the strict discipline. He worked hard academically but did not distinguish himself at sport. The school played Rugby and he was always in the lowest games.

Even at this time Michael was noted for his goodness of character. To the Chileans at the Grange he was *el Gringo bueno.* For Latin Americans to this day it is common to lump white Europeans and white North Americans together as *Gringos*. Most of the English-speaking boys at the Grange were Anglican. Under the rules of the Catholic Archbishop of Santiago, Cardinal Caro, Catholic children were forbidden to attend Protestant schools and Catholic priests were consequently not permitted to provide religious instruction in these schools. The Grange got round this ban by acquiring the services of young theology students from the Catholic University of Santiago who came in and gave Religion lessons to its Catholic boys. Later, during Michael's time, the rules were relaxed and, for several years, the saintly Fr Alberto Hurtado, a Jesuit priest and champion of the poor, thought to be a candidate for canonization, taught Religion at the Grange.[3]

In 1947, when the War and its immediate after-effects were over and Roy's posting in Chile was coming to an end, preparations were made to transfer Michael and John to a Public School in England and, preferably, to one which was Catholic. Mary had a cousin living in London whose son was a boarder at Downside School, near Bath, in Somerset. On the Woodwards' behalf her husband, Fred Lesser, wrote to the Headmaster in February 1947, asking that Michael and John be accepted for the following September as a special concession in view of the short notice. He explained that if it had not been for the War, Roy 'would have sent his two boys home here to school some time ago'.[4] In spite of his fifteen years upbringing in Chile, 'home' for Michael was still considered by his father to be England.

Downside was an English Public School of the sort that The Grange prepared its pupils for, but unlike most of them in being run by English Benedictine monks exclusively for the sons of Catholics. The new Headmaster, Dom Wilfrid Passmore, was energetically building up the numbers and academic results of the

School from the low point they had reached at the end of the War. Under his direction Downside was within nine years to reach first place in Great Britain in the league table of entry awards to the Universities of Oxford and Cambridge. The unexpected arrival of two intelligent boys from South America might help his plans and was therefore welcome. He informed Roy Woodward, however, that he was making places for them as a favour in view of Mr Lesser's recommendation and proposed that the boys should do an intensive Latin course during their remaining time at The Grange to prepare themselves for Downside. Roy was not happy with this: 'They are both rather keen on science and such-like things', he wrote, 'and it is our idea that they should take the modern side of subjects'.[5] Dom Wilfrid replied informing him that Latin was necessary not only for admission to any English University but also for the professions of lawyer, doctor or accountant. Roy gave way and Michael and John both studied Latin during their remaining months at The Grange. In the reference he sent to Downside when Michael left, the Headmaster of The Grange wrote: 'Throughout his time with us Michael's work has been excellent, and he has generally been very near the top, if not top of his form. He is clever, capable and industrious. His conduct has also been excellent. He is reserved and has a pleasant disposition. He is honourable and correct'.[6]

Michael's and John's transfer to an English boarding school came at a convenient moment since it coincided with Roy's new posting by British American Tobacco to Rio de Janeiro, which he would take up in January 1948. Before settling there he, Mary and three of the children made the journey by sea to Europe. Leaving the port of Valparaiso on 31st July 1947, they sailed north to the Panama Canal and on to New York which they reached on 21st August. Roy, ever practical, thought the time in New York would be useful since 'clothes are easy to come by there' (they were still rationed in the UK) 'and possibly of better quality and cheaper than here (Chile). It will also do the children good to have a few days to look round New York'. By 3rd September the family were in London. The following week they drove to Mayfield in Sussex where Jocelyn was to become a boarder with the Holy Child nuns and, the next day, travelled to Somerset. Roy and Mary had an interview with Dom Wilfrid who showed them round the School. A few days later Michael and John travelled from London on the School train to start their first term at Downside.

Michael *(right)* & John on their way to school in England, 1947

Correspondence about clothing coupons to cover the brothers' needs for sportswear and other items of school uniform and a letter from Dom Wilfrid requesting Roy's consent to their Confirmation in November 1947, are the only records of their first term. The Christmas vacation was spent with the whole family skiing at Adelboden in Switzerland. Fred Lesser was appointed official guardian in the United Kingdom to Michael and John now that their parents would be living in Brazil. Care was taken in finding suitable lodging for the boys' subsequent school holidays and the home of a Commander and Mrs Stokes at Godstone Court in Surrey, was chosen. The boys spent two holidays there and were evidently happy since they wished to return for the following Christmas.[7]

In the summer of 1948 Michael took his School Certificate, gaining four distinctions (English Language, Spanish, Physics and Chemistry) and three credits (English Literature, French, Elementary Maths). Physics, Chemistry and Maths became the most obvious choice of subjects for the Higher Certificate. The following April Dom Wilfrid wrote to Roy about Michael's future. Oxford and Cambridge were ruled out since he had not after all kept up his Latin at Downside. 'He might well prefer to attend a South American University, but the wisdom of this course would depend on the future plans which you have for him and the country in which he is to make his career'. Such deference to the right of parents to determine their son's career sounds odd today, but was normal at a time when people were legally dependent on their parents until the age of 21. It also gave considerable power to the Headmaster who was *in loco parentis*. Respect for the individuality and wishes of children did not come to prevail in the majority of middle-class families until after the social changes of the 1960s. Of his personality the letter continues: 'He is still rather on the quiet side but he is very well mannered and, so far as I can judge, perfectly happy. He makes a very good impression on all those with whom he comes into contact and I am very pleased with him'. Michael was indeed by this time a popular member of his House and School, much liked by his contemporaries for his genial disposition and humour. Though not much of a Rugby or Cricket player, he held his own at Tennis. He and his Anglo-

Peruvian friend, Tom Harrington, a formidable pair, both over six feet tall, won several Tennis competitions for their House.

In July 1949 Michael passed his Higher Certificate in Maths, Physics and Chemistry and was appointed a House Prefect for the following School year. The summer holidays were spent with the family in Rio de Janeiro. Roy wrote to Dom Wilfrid on 9th September: 'It has been great having the children over here, and I must say that both Mary and I are extremely pleased with them and their development'. In September 1949 he returned to school with the aim of gaining distinctions in his subjects for entry to Imperial College, London, where it was planned that he would study either Civil or Electrical Engineering.

In January 1950 an application was made for entry to Imperial College but was turned down: too many applicants for the places available. Michael was competing with mature candidates who had done two years' National Service from which, as a British subject domiciled abroad, he himself was exempt up to the age of 21. Approaches were then made to the Engineering Departments at King's College, London and at the Universities of Bristol and Birmingham. On the 29th April 1950, Dom Wilfrid informed Fred Lesser that 'with very great difficulty I have persuaded the Dean of the Faculty of Engineering at King's College to consider Michael's case'. An interview took place on the 8th May, after which the Dean reported to Dom Wilfrid: 'I am glad to inform you that I have found a place for Mr M.R.Woodward who made a favourable impression at the interview. Fifty boys were selected out of some four hundred applicants'. In the knowledge that he could start working for a B.Sc. in Engineering at King's College, London, the following October, Michael left Downside and flew with John and Jocelyn to rejoin his parents in Rio on the 24th July 1950.

On 11th August, from Brazil, Michael sent the first of a number of letters to his former Headmaster. One item he mentions for Dom Wilfrid's amusement is interesting in view of later controversies with the Bishop of Valparaiso:

> The subject of women's dress in church and on the beach in particular, which you touched on in last term's Religious Instruction, has been taken up with great determination by most parish priests here. Many a sermon is preached against the modern trend in ladies' fashions. One rather venerable priest was heard to say (to his congregation) one Sunday: 'Could you imagine the Virgin Mary on the beach in one of your bathing suits!'

A letter to Dom Wilfrid written in the middle of his second year at Kings, in February 1952, contains the first surviving reference to a religious vocation. It is evidently something which Michael had been pondering for some time and had previously confided to his Headmaster: 'As to my future, I am sticking to my vocation, but am still uncertain as to whether to become a Regular or Secular priest. With me this is a knotty problem'. He proposes a visit to Downside with his newly married uncle and aunt to see John, now a prefect, and so that they could inspect the School since they were 'almost prospective parents'. Michael adds 'I will show them only the most modern parts of the school'. Dom Wilfrid replied by return: 'I should very much like to discuss everything with you and to help you to clear your mind and I shall, therefore, keep myself entirely at your disposal'. It can be assumed that the discussion took place sometime during the weekend of the 23-24th February, but there is no record of what transpired.

A letter in May 1952 asks Dom Wilfrid for help in finding some contact in the shipping world through whom

Michael might be able to work his passage to Rio instead of flying. 'My father is willing to pay my air passage to Brazil this summer, but this will entail a tremendous expense as John and Peter are also flying over there'. In the event the initiative came to nothing because, as he wrote, in spite of being given a contact, 'working a passage, I have now learnt, is a very difficult proposition these days, so I have had to give up the idea for this year. I began trying too late'.

Instead, he flew out to Rio once more. He adds: 'The second year exams were reasonable; fortunately our internal examiners did not exert their imaginations unduly when setting the papers. So perhaps all will be well'. He sends his kind regards to the Abbot of Downside (Dom Christopher Butler) which suggests that by this time they were acquainted. In all probability Michael had discussed his vocation with him on a previous visit and perhaps even considered trying it in the Monastery at Downside. At all events he paid a further visit to Downside at short notice before the end of the summer term.

In the early part of 1953, during his last year at King's, Michael wrote to Dom Wilfrid saying that he looked forward 'to seeing you and attending what will be my first Annual Reunion. Ever since I learnt History under Dom Lucius during my first term at School, I have always wanted to hear him sing *Clementine*. I hope he is still in good voice'. This refers to the annual reunion of Alumni of the School during Holy Week, from Maundy Thursday evening until Easter Sunday, during which the visitors attended the Holy Week services and listened to retreat talks. The Reunion ended with a celebratory lunch on Easter Sunday at which the aged monk, Dom Lucius Graham, a long-standing History teacher in the School, always sang *Clementine*.[8]

In May 1953, Roy Woodward was in London staying at the Park Lane Hotel. It may have been a business visit, but he also had anxieties concerning his eldest son. On 18th May, he sent a handwritten letter to Dom Wilfrid asking to see him at Downside on the following Sunday 'regarding Michael, who, as you know, is set on becoming a Trappist,[9] while I consider he could help people so much more elsewhere'. An offspring's desire to join a monastery of strict observance where he would be cut off from the outside world and from his own family would be hard for most parents to accept. For Roy, with his severely practical outlook, it was probably incomprehensible. Dom Wilfrid agreed to see Roy on 24th May but pressure of appointments allowed for only a very brief interview of which no record survives. Probably he reassured Roy that a dose of first hand experience of the Trappist way of life would put Michael off the idea, but if his desire were to survive the experience of a trial period, his vocation to the Cistercians was to be taken seriously.

Michael did indeed go on a visit to Caldey Abbey, the Trappist monastery on an island off the coast of Pembrokeshire. In a brief letter written to Dom Wilfrid on the 22nd June, he says:

> Over Whitsun I went down to Caldey to see the Prior and, as you suggested, he recommended me to stay here for a time as a period of trial. I have just arrived and am staying until July 16th. On the 18th John and I leave for Brazil. I am still not certain in my own mind whether the contemplative life would be the best for God's service in my case. These three weeks following will be decisive. My engineering course is over; the results of the exams will not be announced until the 15th July. We have celebrated them in advance.

In his reply, dated 24th June 1953, Dom Wilfrid reminds Michael that

... the ultimate responsibility for the next step rests with you. If you do not see the way clearly, then I think you ought to reconsider the whole matter. It seems to me that a religious vocation is very similar to being in love. Nothing will stop a person who is in love from obtaining his object, and so it is with those who are called to the Religious life. Nevertheless, the Cistercian life makes exceptionally heavy demands upon those who seek to enter it, and I do not think that you should embrace it without a deep conviction that this is the way for you and with the full approval and encouragement of the Superiors at Caldey.

The outcome of his stay at Caldey was made known in a letter written to Dom Wilfrid on the 19th July 1953, on board the *Uruguay Star*:

John and I are on our way home to Rio for the summer vacation. My course of Engineering is now over. I managed to obtain a pass degree. I was very much impressed by the life at Caldey; I did not find it as hard as I expected. At the moment, though, I feel that I would rather use my head than my hands, and should, therefore, not join the Cistercians where only manual work is done.

Next September I shall be going, on the advice of the Prior of Caldey, to Campion House, Osterley, the college for late vocations run by the Jesuits. There I shall learn Latin, Greek and English, for a year or perhaps two, since whatever Order I join, some grounding in Latin is necessary. During that year I will be able to look around and see the different Orders of the Church and decide which to enter. I have heard Campion House is quite a mixing ground; you meet all kinds of candidates for the priesthood, which is a good thing. I hope the Jesuits will 'let me out' on occasions and I shall certainly visit you at Downside next year.

In a further letter written on the 3rd January 1954, from

14

Campion House, Michael communicated the result of his deliberations:

> I have decided finally to join the ranks of the Secular Clergy out in Chile. I think it is a natural step for me to take as I was born and bred out there. Also the shortage of priests is even graver than in most countries. I have written to the Bishop of Valparaiso and he has unofficially accepted me, so I am preparing to leave England in early February in order to enter the Seminary there in March. Seminarians, other than those direct from the Junior Seminary, learn Latin in conjunction with the three year Philosophy course, so there's no difficulty in that direction. Latin is not taught at any Chilean school. I had a very profitable term at Campion House, and the Latin and Greek I learnt there will be very useful in Chile.

He paid one last visit to Downside and Fr Wilfrid on the weekend of the 23rd-24th January 1954 and left England early in the following month.

NOTES

1. For the facts concerning Michael's family and childhood I am indebted to his sister Jocelyn Henfrey and brother, John Woodward. Interpretative observations are my own, unless in quotation marks.
2. Mariano Puga 1990.
3. ibid., confirmed 1996.
4. All the correspondence quoted in this chapter is from the Downside School archives.
5. Letter from Roy Woodward, 7th March 1947.
6. Letter from John Jackson to Dom Wilfrid, 16th August 1947.
7. Later on they stayed with or near a school friend, Freddy Ball, who also had South American connections.
8. Sadly, on this particular occasion, Easter Sunday 1953, Dom Lucius sang *Clementine* for the last time and died of heart failure immediately afterwards.
9. The Trappists are an order of reformed Cistercian monks following the *Rule of St Benedict* on what are considered to be the strictest lines.

CHAPTER TWO

PREPARATION (1954-1963)

On the 8th March, 1954, Michael, now in Viña del Mar, Chile, once more wrote to his former Headmaster, Dom Wilfrid Passmore:

> England seems quite remote from this corner of the world. Most people here know little about it and the popular representation of an Englishman is a tall, fair, well groomed gentleman who smokes a pipe, eats an enormous breakfast and says little. The environment here is totally different, as I expected, but with time I hope to feel thoroughly at home. I had an interview with the Bishop of Valparaiso, the Diocese where I was born and lived for fifteen years, and he accepted me, so that I shall be entering the seminary on March 21st. He told me there was a tremendous shortage of priests: in Chile with a population of six million nominal Catholics there are only four hundred and fifty Chilean priests. Seminarians with degrees in Engineering are no novelty here: there are four engineers from my Diocese who are now reading Theology.

He had met up with his old school friend, Freddy Ball, who was working with a British firm in Chile, and their 'thoughts immediately went back to Downside, the good old days'.[1]

The Pontifical Seminary in Santiago,[2] which Michael entered as a student on 21st March, was virtually the national seminary for the whole of Chile. The course of studies consisted of two years of Philosophy, four of Theology and a final year of pastoral theory and practice. The Rector, Alberto Rencoret, had taken over, the same term that Michael entered, from Emilio Tagle, who was later to be Michael's Bishop in Valparaiso.

The seminary had approximately a hundred and twenty students, eighty in Philosophy and forty in Theology. Whether the smaller number in the senior section was due to wastage and weeding out or a sudden increase in entries is not clear, probably a bit of both: in these pre-Vatican II years under Pope Pius XII, the Catholic Church was attracting many vocations to the priesthood. Michael's year was twenty-two strong to start with, eight of them coming from the Diocese of Valparaiso. It included some powerful, creative characters who gained fame or notoriety, according to the viewpoint of the judgment, and was remembered long after, for reasons which will become clear, as the 'Year of the Circus'. Many of them were mature students: that is to say, like Michael, they were already university graduates and had not simply moved up, as was more usual, from a

Michael *(standing, centre)* with his family, 1950

minor seminary. These university graduates had minds of their own and were unlikely to accept authority uncritically. Michael was the sole member of his year who had been educated abroad. Most of his contemporaries felt themselves called to the priesthood as a consequence of their involvement in one of the forms of Catholic Action, whether with factory workers, rural labourers or fellow university students.

The seminary was a hundred years old and due to be replaced after Michael's first year when they moved into a new building, commissioned by the former Rector, Emilio Tagle, in a well-to-do, residential district of Santiago. Conditions in the old building were primitive. Michael's old friend from The Grange School, Mariano Puga, woke on his first morning at seminary with wet hair from a leaking roof. When he mentioned this to the Rector, he was told to move his bed. Students' opinions of the seminary food varied: all found it indifferent; some thought it inadequate. For breakfast there was tasteless porridge with milk and *ersatz* coffee. Philosophy students, especially those in their first year, who were not yet accustomed to the meagreness of the diet, ate the bread left over by the Theology students. The new Seminarians slept in a large dormitory divided into single compartments. The floor shook when people ran down the central passage way. The showers were reached by crossing an outside courtyard. Hot showers were available briefly on a Wednesday afternoon. There were only three of them, heated by a coal furnace which produced more steam than hot water. The cleanest Seminarians were those who ran fastest. By Thursday morning the water was tepid and thereafter it was cold. The new seminary boasted much better facilities: each room had its own shower. But the students still suffered from the cold because there were not enough funds to operate the central heating. The football and basketball pitches were unfinished for the same reason and there were facilities for showing films but no money to hire them.

Seminary life was cut off from the outside world. Students could have one day out a month, though those who came from Valparaiso were allowed to leave early on a Saturday morning and return late on Sunday. On other Saturdays they went out in the afternoon to perform some kind of apostolate in a poor district (*poblacion*), usually catechesis or the preparation of children for First Communion. The month of January was spent relaxing at the seminary's summer residence on the coast at Punta de Tralca.[3] The students spent February at home with their families. Michael stayed with his grandmother in Viña, where his family also came each year for a holiday, until she died in 1962. From then on he had no close family left in Chile. During this summer leave the Seminarians undertook some part-time apostolate of their own choosing. Michael helped Student Catholic Action groups with their summer camps for slum children. With his friends, Pato Guarda and Pepo Gutierrez, he was also involved in running a Catholic cine club with discussions afterwards.

If conditions in the seminary were austere, Michael made light of them. His own health was not robust. He became severely run down after any cold and may have suffered from low blood pressure. The authorities arranged for him to be put on a special diet. In view of his height, jokes were made about the food not reaching his head, for sometimes he would lose his train of thought, doubtless through lack of oxygen to the brain. One Lent, when his self-imposed penances were added to the general austerity, he had to ask his friend Mariano Puga to tie his shoe laces for him when he got up in the morning: he couldn't remember how to do it himself. His friends urged him to take care of his health but he paid no attention.

In his early days at the seminary, Michael was punctilious in his conduct: always impeccably dressed in his cassock, studious during work periods and scrupulous at keeping the rules of silence. When fellow students teased him about this, he saw the joke, laughed and carried on as before. They thought him very English. In fact he was not comfortable in the Spanish language and committed solecisms such as using the word *caballa* (an imaginary feminine form of *caballo* - a horse) instead of *yegua* (the correct word for a mare). But he was anxious to assimilate and become as Chilean as possible. On one of his summer holidays in Viña he took with him and read a large *History of Chile*.[4]

At this time Michael was more interested in catechising the young and training lay people for the apostolate than in the social and economic problems of Chile. He may, however, have had an early introduction to the concept of class struggle. One of the students in his year, Roberto Romero, had been a factory worker before joining the seminary and suggested to his fellow students that they were bourgeois intellectuals. He attracted Michael's admiration, but the friendship which grew up between them did not at this stage lead into politics. It remained within a framework of religious piety: they prayed together in the Sodality of Our Lady of which they were both members.[5]

Within Michael's traditional piety there is evidence of a developing awareness of the marginalised poor of Chile. In a letter written in June 1956, 'on the feast of the Sacred Heart' to a cousin in Viña, he says: 'Christ's Church is the Church of all people, but especially the Church of the poor. We have to become closer to them, not as if doing them a favour, but as a simple and natural expression of brotherly love'.[6] His view of the apostolate (exercised from the seminary on Saturday afternoons) is expressed in another letter to his cousin at this time:

> I have the task of teaching a group of seven- to nine-year-old girls. They have recently made their first Confession. And like you I also have to visit the homes of their parents. As you say, it is necessary to speak about God, but I would say myself that it is important to win the family's trust, to be really interested in their problems — they all have them — and through this friendly contact and through listening to their problems to come to speak about God. This is the most natural and human way to conduct an apostolate, given how far the people are from any kind of true Christianity.

In the same letter he speaks of a discussion in the seminary on Pius XII's encyclical *Sacra Virginitas*, on priestly celibacy: 'This Encyclical is terrific. It has given me a real understanding of evangelical purity, that is to say total self-consecration to God out of love for Him alone. Chastity is thus something positive and noble, and something fundamental in the religious vocation: it is the living expression of a complete abandonment of oneself to God'. Such was his fervour that, during one of his annual holidays at his grandmother's in Viña, Michael decided to give up all his worldly goods. Exactly what they consisted of and how he disposed of them is not recorded. He also had all his family praying the Rosary at home on their return from the beach.[7]

In his studies Michael did not diligently accept at face value everything that was given to him: he delved into those areas which interested him but was critical of much of the teaching. He was not alone in regarding the Scripture course as unsatisfactory, but was interested enough to do some independent reading. In particular, a

21

work by Xavier Leon-Dufour prompted him to put questions to the Scripture lecturers on salvation history: he was not satisfied by their replies. Most of the university graduates in the seminary had been involved in the Young Christian Worker movement and consequently were interested in the social teachings of the Church. By now Michael's interest in this area had also been aroused: he was glad to hear the lectures on this subject by the Professor of Moral Theology, Fr Jose Aldunate SJ,[8] but found the three weeks allowed for it insufficient.

Michael's contemporaries remember the Rector, Alberto Rencoret, as a man of great kindness who made a point of building up the self-confidence of any students who felt unsure of themselves. He had a special attachment to Michael's year. He had himself been a Young Christian Worker chaplain and in his monthly meetings with the year group used to discuss how Christian theology could be adapted to the language of the world of labour. Rencoret was concerned that his future priests should preach the Gospel with their lives and especially urged poverty as their lifestyle. He forged close links with the Little Brothers of Jesus, the religious congregation inspired by the life and spirituality of Charles de Foucauld. The students regularly spent half days of recollection with them. The founder and leader of the Little Brothers, René Voillaume, visited the seminary.

Rencoret was keen on the Little Brothers' ideal of 'incarnation' — living among poor people and on equal terms with them. Like the Son of God himself, Rencoret's Seminarians were truly to dwell among the ordinary and poor people they served. There was no question of their becoming priests for prestige or money. To identify with the rich was a scandal. His was a spirituality of the presence of Christ in the poor.

A frequent visitor to the seminary was Manuel Larrain, Bishop of Talca, founder of the Episcopal

22

Conference of Latin America (CELAM). It was he who initiated the Chilean Church's own land reform and became internationally famous as the first Latin American bishop to hand his episcopal palace over to the homeless. Under such influences, Michael and his friends at the seminary learned to look beyond themselves and their own milieu, planned to commit themselves in their future ministry to those members of Chilean society who found themselves at the bottom of the heap, and to avoid becoming enmeshed in a self-regarding, middle-class, ecclesiastical world.

Carlos Gonzalez, who succeeded Rencoret as Rector in 1957 and also had a considerable influence on Michael and his contemporaries, was himself a member of the Jesus Caritas Fraternity of priests. This was — and is — an association of diocesan priests who try to live their daily lives according to the spirituality of de Foucauld, a sort of priestly Third Order of the Little Brothers of Jesus. With its emphasis on eucharistic adoration, simplicity of life and the sharing of experience with the brethren in a 'Review of Life', the Jesus Caritas Fraternity was the model for the 'Life Teams' which operated in the seminary and which were an attempt to combat what was seen as clerical individualism. Each student intake was divided into several groups of four or five. In the early years the groups were chosen by the authorities, but in Theology the students chose their own. These teams would take responsibility for various tasks which were part of seminary life, such as arranging the Liturgy, but they were also intended to be a source of mutual support and companionship.

Life at the seminary included some lighter moments. *Fiesta* in Spanish means both a holy day, or Solemnity, and a party and, on certain special occasions, the two were very properly combined on the same day. On one such day, the patronal feast of the Guardian

Angels in October 1954, it fell to Michael's year group to organise the accompanying party. They decided to make it a 'Circus' and, as an advance publicity stunt, Michael and his friends performed the considerable feat of manhandling a car into the Refectory for the festal meal. For the Circus itself they persuaded a passing cart driver in the street to lend them a horse which made its appearance, ridden by a greatly overweight Seminarian wearing a turban and minuscule swimming trunks. The Seminarian departed not long afterwards.

Michael and his friend Pepo Gutierrez were dressed as clowns. Michael was thrown an orange which he in turn threw into the air and caught, then a second, which he also threw up and caught in the same hand as the first. It was an exhibition of how not to juggle. He maintained a dead-pan expression. Eventually he was thrown ten oranges which he caught in his arms. Then, after thinking about juggling with the lot, he shrugged his shoulders and threw them away into the audience, maintaining a dignified detachment throughout

The juggling was followed by a flea hunt. One of the clowns provoked an invisible flea to jump from one of his hands to the other and back again This was repeated several times before the flea escaped. There followed a feverish hunt in which either the original flea or its increasingly numerous companions were discovered among the tonsures of the seated professors and ecclesiastical dignitaries. There was also a joke in poorer taste which involved sticking a communion host on to the back of a Seminarian's head as a tonsure. The atmosphere froze. Carlos Camus, head of the year and later to be Bishop of Linares, was severely admonished.

Such horseplay at the expense of the teaching staff and visiting clergy was not entirely innocent. It was coloured by the reaction of the students of Michael's year, men who had been out and experienced ordinary

24

University life, to what they saw as the petty rules of the seminary. For instance, there was a rule that trousers should not be visible below the cassock These were still the days when cassocks, shovel hats and gloves were worn by clerical students. No contact was permitted between Philosophy students and Theology students. A certain mark on the floor of the corridor linking their two sections of the building designated the boundary which no student was permitted to cross. The Prefect of Theology and canon lawyer, Jorge Medina,[9] was considered particularly rigid and stuffy. There was a dog, a kind of seminary mascot, which he objected to and had put down. Perhaps partly on account of this there was tension between Medina and the students of Michael's year and they enjoyed taunting him. When Medina insisted on absolute silence, a bugle was blown loudly and passed on a string from window to window while Medina hurried from room to room searching for the culprit. When he made a fuss about the importance of Seminarians wearing a clerical collar at all times, Pepo Gutierrez appeared in public wearing a collar and nothing else.

Michael's yearly reports starting from the end of his first year in Theology have survived in the Valparaiso Diocesan archives. In December 1956, one professor referred to him as 'notoriously pious'. Another states: 'I have been aware of his great desire to be a priest'. Jorge Medina, on the same date, says of him: 'He is straightforward and humble, endowed with extraordinary natural kindness'. In the same report, rectitude is singled out among his 'natural virtues'. His relations with fellow Seminarians are described as straight-forward and kindly, those with his teachers as obedient and humble: it all sounds un-perceptive and idealised, a stereotype based on superficial observation and couched in the preferred categories of the day. His emotional development is described as 'normal'. He has a 'spirit of sacrifice' and 'apostolic motivation' evidenced by his fidelity to 'his Catechism classes' — presumably the Saturday afternoon visits to a *poblacion* to prepare young people for First Communion. His studies reveal ability and application (marks average five out of seven). Some concern is expressed that he needs extra food because of his stature. He is 'making efforts to adapt to Chilean ways'. Lastly there is a heading marked 'weaknesses' under which appears the phrase 'somewhat rigid'.

On 6th April 1957, Michael received the tonsure in Valparaiso Cathedral. In his report that year, his work as Assistant Librarian is commended as 'responsible and efficient'. His distinctive qualities are enumerated as 'supernatural, sensitive and hard-working'. But at the same time he is 'somewhat obstinate' and concern is expressed about 'a certain lack of adaptation deriving from his foreign background'. It is recommended that he be given opportunities to become better assimilated to the environment in which he will carry out his apostolate. In retrospect his fellow student and head of year, who was closer to him at the time than the seminary staff, says of him: 'He was always quiet. He didn't express his feelings much. He was shy, reserved and, I believe, very prayerful: a spiritual person sensitive to friendship. He was grateful when you approached him for a chat because he found it difficult to get close to others. He was sensitive and very shy. The rest of his year were great talkers, but he was much loved. When we had to give reports on him we always singled out his piety and kindness. He was always available for the sick'.[10]

On 22nd March 1958, Michael received the minor orders of Door-keeper and Reader in Valparaiso Cathedral and the next day those of Exorcist and Acolyte in the Chapel of the Carmelite Sisters of the Sacred Heart in Viña del Mar. In his report on this occasion Jorge Medina again expressed concern about Michael's

26

Englishness: 'His personality as a whole reflects very strongly his English descent and education. These, together with a certain shyness, may later on become something of an obstacle to his apostolate. I believe that he shows genuine promise of becoming a good priest'. Another member of staff echoes the same concern: 'He really must try to adapt to the Chilean mentality and overcome his tendency to be carried away by Anglo-Saxon rigidity which may make it difficult for him to get on with people'.

Michael's final report, dated 9th April 1960, reveals his academic preferences: Out of a maximum of seven marks each, for Old Testament he gained six, for New Testament seven, five each for Dogmatic Theology and Canon Law, for Moral Theology four. Under the heading 'natural virtues' reservation is expressed about his judgment which 'lacks realism'. Under 'modesty': generally satisfactory, but 'somewhat arrogant in his opinions'. A similar point is made under 'weaknesses': 'rather stubborn and extreme; he has a tendency to criticize without being actually censorious'. He is commended for his genuine and relatively successful efforts to adapt and is seen as having 'a priestly face'. His relations with superiors are described as good: 'He is sincere and obedient even when it goes against the grain'. It sounds as if some of his teachers were disconcerted by his criticisms but attributed them to the fact that he was English and not Chilean. They could not but be impressed by his religious motivation.

Jorge Medina's final report on Michael, referring as it does to unspecified clashes between the two of them, reveals a certain hesitation in recommending him to his Bishop for Major Orders:

> He is a very serious and conscientious Seminarian, studious and dutiful. He is pious and zealous for the apostolate, especially with working people, and shows

special interest in Biblical studies. On a number of occasions he has shown how difficult it is for him to be obedient; he is quite persistent in his own opinions. This has prompted several warnings to him to concentrate a little more on humility. His tendency to be critical has led him occasionally into a disrespectful attitude towards the writer of this report, but without descending into a general climate of hostility. All in all, basing myself principally on his genuine motivation and piety, I believe that he shows promise of being a good priest and that it is right for him to proceed to the Subdiaconate. It would be a good idea, however, to speak seriously to him about the weaknesses I have mentioned and on the repercussions they might have on the life of the Diocese.

On the 11th June 1960, having taken the anti-Modernist oath, he was ordained to the Subdiaconate by Mgr Raul Silva Henrique. His fellow ordinands for the Diocese of Valparaiso, were Pepo Gutierrez (to the diaconate) and Patricio Guarda (to the subdiaconate). Three months later, on 24th September, Michael was ordained Deacon.

During this period of the subdiaconate and diaconate Michael gained pastoral experience working in a parish. A young priest, Wenceslao Barra, who supervised him for part of this time, in his report on Michael, offers the kinder and more perceptive interpretation of a near-contemporary:

Pious, desiring to dedicate himself totally to the Church. Thoughtful, in an analytical way. Broad general culture. Above average intellectual curiosity and ability. Special interest in Biblical theology. Slow in his thought processes, which can be mistaken for stubbornness. Reserved in personal matters. In general I think highly of him.

On 25th February 1961, after a six day retreat at Punta de Tralca, Michael was ordained Priest by Bishop Raul Silva Henrique in the Cathedral of Our Lady of Mount Carmel in Valparaiso. The Woodward family were there and the Cathedral was full of people from the *poblaciones* where Michael had done pastoral work as a deacon. His sister, who was present, had the impression that 'Michael definitely belonged to them'[11]

How Michael spent the seven months following his ordination is not clear. He almost certainly stayed with his parents in Sao Paulo, Brazil, before going to Europe. In September 1961 he was in London to celebrate the wedding of his sister Jocelyn. The following month he started a two year post-graduate course at the Institut Superieur de Catechétique, part of the Institut Catholique, in Paris. Whose idea it was that he should do this course is not known, but it must have had the approval of Bishop Silva. For newly ordained priests who were capable of University level studies, it was normal to do a stint in Europe if they had not already done so before ordination.

Perhaps with a view to adapting himself better to the mentality of those he would serve as a priest, Michael chose to concentrate on Catechetics. The course included sections on the 'Psychology of Contemporary Man' and 'Christian Anthropology' as well as others more specifically concerned with the theory and practice of Catechesis. The report on him at the end of his time at the Institute is complimentary but bland: 'Father Woodward has brought his studies at the Institute to a satisfactory completion. With his open mind and intellectual curiosity he has greatly profited from his time in France. His warmth and friendliness earned him the esteem and cooperation of his colleagues'. It would be good to know something of the directions in which he was led by his open mind and intellectual curiosity, but on this the report is silent. One external detail from this time is known which clearly suggests some inner change: he now dressed, not in a cassock — which is not surprising for it would have looked odd by the early sixties on the streets of Paris — not, like most French priests, in a clerical suit and black tie, but in a leather jacket.[12]

While he was in Paris Michael stayed with the Franciscan Missionaries of Mary in Vanves. During his time there he went to London to preside at his brother John's wedding at St Mary's, Cadogan Street. Gonzalo Aguirre, a contemporary and friend from the seminary was in London at the time and met up with him. For this occasion he had to dress conventionally and the two of them caused amusement to onlookers, both wearing clerical suits and collars, one six foot four inches tall, the other five foot two.[13]

Another visit to London was made in October 1962, for the wedding of his younger sister Pat at St Ethelreda's, Ely Place. He joined his family in London several days before the wedding and, according to his younger sister, appeared happy and enthusiastic. She thought, nevertheless, that with his family by this time he was 'like a foreigner'. The path he had chosen was quite alien to them.[14]

On his return to Chile. in late 1963 his contemporary, Carlos Camus, noticed that he was different. 'He arrived back full of enthusiasm: according to him, priestly formation had been totally changed; all that we had learned was outdated scholasticism and now he had discovered a completely new theology. I wondered what they had taught him in Paris'.[15]

There are two interpretations of what is generally agreed was a major change in Michael during his time in France.

> I believe that he underwent strong Marxist influence in Paris, because Dario Marcotti who went with him entered the Communist Party on his return. We

suspected that the French Communist Party paid special attention to students from Latin America, starting with Camilo Torres. We believed they ran a service under the leadership of a Chilean lady called Marta Harnecker who had been in Catholic Action before joining the Communist Party. It was a time of much interchange and nearly all the Chilean priests who went to France were influenced by this woman. They were invited to Moscow, to Christian-Marxist dialogues. They nearly all left the priesthood.[16]

Another friend and contemporary from seminary days, however, denied that Michael changed ideologically during his time in Paris, denied that he came under any particular Communist influence: he simply discovered some good theology.[17]

NOTES

1. Downside School Archives.
2. For details of life at the seminary I am indebted to Michael's fellow student and friend, Mariano Puga and to his head of year, Carlos Camus.
3. It later became a retreat house run by the Sacred Heart Fathers
4. Pat Bennetts 1990
5. Gonzalo Aguirre 1992
6. Letter to Carlos Barhoilet
7. Pat Bennetts 1990
8. Fr Jose Aldunate SJ was, like Michael, an Anglo-Chilean. He was educated at Stonyhurst College, Lancashire. At the age of 55 he gave up teaching to become a priest-worker and, now in his eighties, he continues to live as a Jesuit in a *poblacion* (1996).
9. Later Bishop of Valparaiso, papal retreat giver to John Paul II and Cardinal Prefect of the Sacred Congregation for Divine Worship.
10. Carlos Camus 1992.
11. Pat Bennetts 1990.
12. Carlos Camus 1992.
13. Gonzalo Aguirre 1992.
14. Pat Bennetts 1990.
15. Carlos Camus 1992.
16. ibid.
17. Gonzalo Aguirre 1992.

Above: Entering the seminary in 1954. *From left, front row:* Pepo Gutiérrez (1st); Michael Woodward (3rd); *seated:* Emilio Tagle (6th); Alberto Rencoret (7th). *On his own, top right:* Mariano Puga.
Below: 25th February 1961. Ordination as priest by Bishop (later Cardinal) Raúl Silva Henríquez.

CHAPTER THREE

JOINING THE DIOCESE (1964-1966)

The port city of Valparaiso was founded by the Spanish Conquistadors early in the sixteenth century on a sheltered coastal strip of fertile land to the north west of Santiago. This 'valley of Paradise' rarely extends more than a few hundred yards from the sea shore before the hills beyond start to rise steeply towards the interior. The town grew in size and importance in the nineteenth century when, with the construction of a harbour and a railway to Santiago, it became the principal commercial port on Chile's two and a half thousand mile coastline. During that century British (most frequently Scottish), German and French entrepreneurs, often the younger sons of the gentry, arrived from Europe to seek their fortune: some of the businesses they established have survived to this day.

The business community created its commercial centre on the narrow plain extending from the harbour northwards parallel to the shore. Behind this plain they built their fine timber houses on the lower slopes of the hills overlooking the commercial city and harbour. It is these painted houses,[1] hanging on the edge of the hills, which give modern Valparaiso its picturesque charm, even though in the twenties and thirties of this century the successors of the wealthy merchants who built them moved along the coast to the neighbouring resort of Viña del Mar. The foreign business communities are commemorated by civic monuments such as the British Arch and by the Protestant Cemetery. The Anglican church, somewhat dilapidated in 1990, now serving a small local congregation, bears witness to the respectability and devotion of former expatriates.

Once the narrow coastal strip was full, the only direction in which Valparaiso could expand was up the hills or *cerros* behind the harbour and commercial centre. What began in the nineteenth century as the construction of fine merchants' houses with views over the sea became, in the twentieth, an urban sprawl of streets, squares, walkways and crude flights of steps, houses and shops, churches, hospitals, schools and colleges. By the 1960s not only was the population of Chile increasing at the ferocious rate of two and a half per cent each year, but there was a massive migration from the country to the cities whose populations grew from forty per cent of the country's total in 1940 to seventy per cent of a vastly increased total in 1970. As the second city in Chile, soon to be overtaken by neighbouring Viña del Mar, (in effect they have become a single urban conglomeration), Valparaiso was in this period receiving its share of the constant flow of rural migrants.

The upper parts of the *cerros* were progressively covered in new settlements,some, like Villa Berlin on Cerro Placeres, planned and solidly built with aid from wealthy European countries, others made up of shanty dwellings of wood and corrugated iron, with no electricity, drainage or running water. The steep gradients of the hills and gullies, the cold winters and high rainfall, turned the un-surfaced roads and paths into mud slides. Fuel for cooking and heating was hard to obtain. There was much unemployment and even more underemployment resulting in poverty, undernourishment, sickness and high infant mortality.

The rapid growth of urban population, the flight from the countryside to the city, the resulting squalor and need, created new responsibilities not only for the Municipal Councils of Valparaiso and Viña, not only for the Conservative-Liberal Government of Jorge Alessandri, President of Chile from 1958 to 1964, but for municipalities and governments throughout Latin America where the same thing was happening. Furthermore, since the independence wars of the early nineteenth century, the United States had considered the whole of Latin America to be rightfully under its political and economic sway, as enunciated in the Monroe Doctrine. In 1959 the corrupt, pro-American regime of General Batista of Cuba was overthrown by the popular revolution of Fidel Castro and the country became a Marxist client state of the Soviet Union. This was a challenge to American dominance of the hemisphere, a challenge which was brought to a climax in 1962 when the Soviet Union under Kruschev attempted to set up a nuclear missile base in Cuba. This provocation was seen off with a dramatic ultimatum by President John F.Kennedy, but the long term threat of Marxist revolution continued to cause anxiety to United States governments. It could erupt in any one of the countries of Latin America where the vast majority of the wealth was held and controlled by a tiny number of families, and an increasingly articulate and politicised working population was beginning to see the inadequacy of the rewards of its own labour by comparison as a scandalous provocation.

United States foreign policy and overseas aid were directed to averting further Marxist revolution in the hemisphere. President Kennedy's Alliance for Progress was devised as one of the ways of pre-empting such an eventuality. It aimed to create economic opportunities, most especially for the rural poor, by pressuring Governments to introduce agrarian reform, breaking up the big estates and giving land to those who worked them. It offered aid for roads and other kinds of infrastructure, and for loans to help small farmers set up business. Another Kennedy invention, The Peace Corps, which provided young volunteers in their twenties from the United States for community service projects in Latin America, was aimed, largely in vain as it turned out, at gaining friends and influence on the Continent.

If the United States Government saw the increasing frustration of the dispossessed populations of Latin America as a threat to the western hemisphere's stability, the Catholic Church saw it both as a challenge of conscience and a threat to its existence. The overwhelming majority of the population of the whole Continent was Catholic: the Soviet Communism which might by democratic or violent means take hold of it was atheistic. Pope John XXIII appealed to the Bishops of Europe and North America to send one fifth of their clergy to Latin America which was chronically short of priests. Many bishops responded to this call, and priests from Europe and North America settled all over the continent, with mixed results.

On his way to the first session of the Vatican Council, in 1962, the new Bishop of Valparaiso, Emilio Tagle, stopped off in Barcelona to ask the local bishop if he had any young clergy to spare for work in his diocese. As a result, a group of five young men, 'the Catalans', as they came to be called, joined the Valparaiso Diocese over the next year to work with the urban poor. Tagle, who at the time was considered progressive, welcomed them warmly. What he did not realise was that, with their hostility to the Franco Regime which had defeated socialism and Catalan nationalism in their own country and their readiness to identify with the poor in their country of adoption, their ideas of what the Church's pastoral strategy should be would conflict radically with his. Although he was from a different background, Michael came to share the ideas of the Catalans and counted some of them among his friends.

Emilio Tagle had been installed as Bishop of Valparaiso in May 1961, replacing Raúl Silva Henríquez who had been appointed as Archbishop of Santiago. Tagle had been picked as Auxiliary Bishop of Santiago by Cardinal Caro and succeeded him as Apostolic

Administrator of the Diocese with the personal title of Archbishop when Caro died in December 1958. The two year delay in choosing a successor suggests that the Vatican hesitated between Tagle and Silva. In the event Pope John XXIII chose as the future Cardinal Archbishop the man who in later years was to become the leading ecclesiastical opponent of the Pinochet Regime and, as Bishop of Valparaiso, the man who was to become its leading ecclesiastical supporter.

From 1947 to 1954 Tagle had been first Spiritual Director, then Rector of the Pontifical Seminary in Santiago, his last days there coinciding with Michael's first. Before that he had worked in parishes in the countryside around Santiago. In one of these he became concerned with the poverty and wretched living conditions of the agricultural workers. He persuaded the local landowners to set up a hardship fund to provide social assistance and financial benefits to needy families. His mother ran a shop from the presbytery to provide them with basic household necessities at cost price. When the Communist and Socialist Parties began to gain strength by unionizing rural workers throughout the country in the late 1930s, Tagle supported the formation of a Catholic rural labour union, the *Union de Campesinos,* which by 1941 had three hundred members in the region where he was working. His support for the Union infuriated the Conservative Party which traditionally considered the Church as its political ally. It put pressure on the bishops to have the Union disbanded.[2]

Tagle worked hard in these years to form Christian labour leaders through the study of Catholic social teaching. It was a time when many of those who later became Christian Democrat politicians were finding their bearings and Tagle played some part in This process. It was from these years that he acquired his reputation for being a progressive.

A man of piety, pastoral zeal and personal charm, Tagle had had a narrow upbringing. Always a model pupil at school, he entered the Seminary at seventeen. The sacrifice of the Mass, the authority of the Pope and devotion to Mary were the core of his spiritual life. Until her death, his mother lived with him permanently and, when she became old and frail, his sister, a Religious of the Sacred Heart, came and looked after them both. She remained with him after their mother died.

In view of his earlier work and influence, Tagle should have been proud when the Christian Democrats became the Government of the country and attempted to change Chilean society for the better. But when it became apparent that the change might become Radical, he took fright and withdrew to the simple moral certainties of the traditional Catholicism of his childhood. Subtlety had little place in his outlook. The military dictatorship of Pinochet offered a clear, paternal authority which would eradicate the 'cancer' of Marxism. That it also eradicated ordinary democratic political rights was a relief to Tagle insofar as these rights raised awkward questions. If, as Bismarck is reputed to have said, democracy is government of the home by the nursery, for all his kindness and compassion towards the children, Tagle was only happy with government by those he considered to be the grown-ups. During the Dictatorship he was treated with great honour and affection by the Regime, but with the exception of his Vicar-General, Jorge Bosagna, he became increasingly isolated from his own clergy and his fellow bishops.[3]

In his address to the people of Valparaiso, delivered in the Cathedral on his arrival as their new bishop, Tagle made a vigorous attack on Marxism which he contrasted with true Christian love. 'The world trusts more in hatred and the class struggle. The Lord demands that we love in such a way that our love becomes the great

38

transformer and sustainer of life. We shall conquer Marxism by showing what can be brought about by justice and love'. Christian love signified 'detachment from earthly goods and an effort to create social structures in which God's plan might be realised'. What, understandably, the bishop failed to see was that his Marxist adversaries were as idealistic and those of his clergy who subscribed to their ideas, were as imbued with Christian love as he was, though by now they must have been more in touch with the daily living conditions of the poor. In the end Marxism would not be defeated and Christian love would not prevail. The democratic process, which includes elements of both, would in time bring about an unsteadily developing compromise between the self-interest of the few and justice for the many. The process would, however, be interrupted and thwarted by the use of military power.

Christian love for the bishop also entailed 'the renunciation of luxuries and frivolities'.[4] Austere in his own personal life, the bishop did his best to extirpate one frivolity, at least, from his diocese. A letter in the correspondence columns of *La Estrella*, the Valparaiso evening newspaper, asks why it is possible to wear the bikini in other places but not in Valparaiso. 'Do we live in modern times or not? Is morality not the same everywhere, or is there more immorality in Valparaiso?' The writer is referring to a ban by Archbishop Tagle on the use of the bikini on the beaches of his diocese under pain of excommunication. The newspaper carries a reply from the Editor telling her that the ban was unlikely to be lifted for the beaches in the Diocese of Valparaiso and advising her to wear her bikini on a beach further down the coast, in the Diocese of Santiago, where it was not a mortal sin to do so.[5]

It is no surprise that Emilio Tagle avoided the meetings of the Chilean and other Latin American Bishops at the Second Vatican Council which he attended between 1962 and 1965 in Rome. He became instead a member of the traditionalist Cardinal Ottaviani's 'Gathering of the Fathers' (*Coetus Patrum*) which opposed all the reforms put forward.[6]   Another member of this group was Archbishop Marcel Lefebvre.   He believed that the Council reforms were heretical and later founded the Society of St Pius X whose members were eventually declared schismatic by John Paul II.   But Tagle himself always remained loyal to the Pope.   When the Council was over, he accepted its rulings including the liturgical reforms which followed, while severely criticizing what he saw as the false and misleading interpretations put on them by some.   In July 1977, Archbishop Lefebvre visited the Diocese of Valparaiso, doubtless in search of friends and new recruits.   Tagle refused to meet him and publicly accused him of wounding the Church by his attack on current papal authority.[7]

To his clergy he made a special appeal: 'As your father and pastor I exhort you to form a perfect community of ideals and action in the love of the one priesthood of Christ.   May the *Presbyterium* around the Bishop be the engine which drives the whole work of the Diocese'.   Though he came to be loved by many, including some opponents, for his straightforwardness and warmth, Tagle's paternalistic view of the relationship between bishop and clergy came to be treated with impatience by many of the younger, University-educated, priests.   They neither agreed with his political views nor regarded him as infallible on other issues.   They belonged to different worlds.   The gap between them was to grow ever wider.

Tagle considered his crowning achievement as bishop to be the establishment in his later years of a new major seminary within his diocese aimed at producing priests of a traditional mould.   But with the progressive priests of the sixties there was a lack of understanding. One of them, a friend of Michael's, speaks of the crisis experienced by the large number of clergy in the diocese who did not agree with the bishop's pastoral approach. They felt a 'lack of contact, of interest and of fatherly affection' on his part, all of which contributed to 'a certain feeling of isolation and loneliness' within the Church. Above all there was a 'lack of comprehension'. This priest worked with Catholic students studying in non-Catholic institutions:

> Once a year we used to make a personal commitment as militants in student Catholic Action. In 1967 I invited Bishop Tagle to come and preach. His train of thought was worlds away from how we approached our commitment. The following year I again invited him, this time giving him a list of suggested points for his homily. He ignored them and once more spoke in a completely different direction. The following year I did not invite him.[8]

Another priest friend of Michael's speaks of the 'complete anarchy' in the Diocese of Valparaiso.

> There were no official meetings of clergy. Groups of priests met spontaneously but there were no regular structures. Years went by without any contact with the bishop. After the occupation of the Catholic University in 1967 the bishop did call a diocesan meeting. But the agenda consisted of a discussion of the moral gravity of the bikini and of the even more skimpy tanga.[9]

It was unlikely that a young, intellectually inclined priest returning from Paris full of the new theology would have much common understanding with his bishop or that either of them, with their reserved temperaments and different backgrounds, would have made great efforts to get to know the other or would have succeeded if they had.

Michael's course at the Institut Catholique finished in July 1963. Sometime later that year he arrived in Valparaiso, but with the difference between the European and South American academic years, the Chilean summer holidays being in January and February, it took him a long time to settle in. Even after he had started, it was some months before he picked up a reasonable workload.

The centre of Valparaiso is the Plaza Victoria, a large square dominated by an enormous baobab tree. On the north side is the Cathedral, a twentieth century neo-classical construction (the diocese was only established in recent times). The exterior is dull, the interior cold and empty. Next door, across a side road, stands an impressive building which houses the diocesan offices, the *Obispado*. This is the administrative centre of the diocese, where its financial and legal affairs were (and are still) conducted by clerical and lay administrators, its charitable and pastoral works coordinated and its archives maintained. At the opposite corner of the Cathedral stood a building known as the Chaplains' house (*casa de Asesores*). It was badly damaged by the 1971 earthquake and was subsequently demolished. The top floor of this building was occupied by six priests most of whom were chaplains to various Catholic youth and student groups. Michael was given a position by the bishop which entailed joining this community.

The group included the Administrator of the Cathedral, chaplains to some local primary schools and colleges and some who were involved with Student Catholic Action in universities. The main element of common life in the house was the midday meal cooked by a woman who came in each day. Bishop Tagle maintained contact at this stage by dropping in from time to time, but he rarely stayed for a meal: he was expected to eat what his mother prepared for him at home. On one occasion he brought the chaplains some lobsters which had been

42

presented to him on a Visitation to the Juan Fernandez Islands, a Chilean Dependency hundreds of miles out in the Pacific Ocean opposite Valparaiso. He did not stay to share them.[10]

Adjusting to this Chilean clerical milieu was difficult for Michael and was probably not something for which he had prepared himself. He frequently used to miss the midday meal and was considered to be 'reserved'.[11] Once again he had difficulty with the language. According to one of those who lived in the same house but knew him only superficially, 'Michael's Spanish was not very good and he thought in English. He was very slow, slow in speech and slow in thought. This created a serious barrier for him in communicating with people. He failed to understand jokes and had to make great efforts to keep up with the Chilean temperament'.[12] It is possible that his grasp of Chilean Spanish had suffered in Paris, but also possible that he was not greatly amused by some of the jokes. In Paris he had imbibed much pastoral and catechetical theory and appeared to have his head in the clouds: 'He was intellectual and his ideas lacked practical common sense. He seemed to live on a different level'.[13]

Michael's difficulties were not eased by the fact that he did not have enough to do and was bored. Such meetings as he attended as a chaplain took place only in the evenings; during the day he was at a loose end. It is not surprising that sleeping problems, which had started at Seminary, became a preoccupation. As a survival technique Michael used the device which had served him well in similar situations: he played the clown, encouraging others to laugh at his eccentricities. A colleague at the house comments 'When he arrived he seemed a bit disoriented. But he got on well with the group. He was teased a good deal. I used to ask him "What's it like up there in the stratosphere?"'[14] Being by far the tallest priest in the diocese, he let himself be placed in the Holy Week processions in the Cathedral alongside the most diminutive member of the clergy.[15] The surreal humour of this would have matched Michael's own feelings towards liturgical pomp and ceremony.

As to his sleeping problems, he explained to a friend in the house, that at the Seminary (the new one to which they moved after his first year) it was the cows in the field outside which had kept him awake. Here in the chaplains' house it was the morning light coming through his inadequate curtains. To remedy this he borrowed some black drapes from the Cathedral sacristy and hung them over his windows.[16] The drapes were apparently those used as decoration for the grander and more expensive funerals in the Cathedral.[17]

The progression from training for the priesthood to active work as a priest is a major step which some new priests do not survive. After years of seminary and institutional life there is a natural desire for autonomy. At the same time a new priest needs adequate, suitable work and the support necessary for doing it. Michael lacked the support. The impression comes across that Emilio Tagle, for all his kindness and good intentions, was never really in touch with Michael and lacked the imagination necessary for dealing with him. Doubtless his thinking was that, because Michael had two University degrees and a post-graduate qualification in Catechetics these should be put to use. A few years in a *poblacion* with an understanding senior colleague might have provided him with a more purposeful start. For that was where his heart lay, even at this early stage.

Michael also lacked the close family support on which his Chilean confrères were able to rely. During 1964 his parents left Sao Paulo and retired to Estoril in Portugal. His brothers and sisters were all in Europe. At the end of the year, he did manage to visit them but the fact remained that they were becoming ever more distant. There were to be only two further visits, in 1966 and 1969.

Over the two and a half years he spent in the chaplains' house Michael picked up work piecemeal, some authorised by the bishop, some for which he volunteered and some, no doubt, off-loaded by his colleagues. He became chaplain to one of the many groups in Valparaiso of the Christian Family Movement, whose purpose was to help people prepare for married life.[18] For a time he worked with the Diocesan Catechetical Institute, forming young catechists for parishes, and he had some limited involvement with Student Catholic Action.

The one post to which he was directly assigned by the bishop was that of Chaplain to the 'Movement of Catholic Professionals'. Oscar Guarda, brother of Michael's seminary friend, Patricio, worked as an engineer in the oil refinery at Con Con (near Valparaiso). As a student himself, he had been involved in University Catholic Action and in 1960, after they started work, he and some friends formed the Movement for Catholic Professionals. They had a chaplain, but he was called to the Vatican Council as a theological adviser and, early in 1963 Emilio Tagle proposed Michael, who himself had a degree in Engineering, to replace him.

The group had about twenty members. Their aim was to make connections between their lives as professionals and as Christians. Most of them worked in industry, some were lawyers, accountants,and doctors. Oscar Guarda describes their objectives: 'We sought ways of serving the poor in our work: by greater participation of the workforce with management, by not forgetting that the workforce were human beings, not machines or conscripts, by creating work so that more might have jobs'.

Michael became very involved in the group. They

met once a week in their respective houses. Most of the members were married with children and meetings would be interrupted by their comings and goings. The procedure developed by the time Michael joined them was to read a passage from a Gospel, or a New Testament letter, and extract such conclusions as seemed appropriate and realistic in their various work situations. The host of the evening chose the reading and expounded it. Discussion followed.

Some evidence of Michael's religious thought and attitudes are provided in the recollections of the group leader:

> Michael thought that working with professionals was not what he was looking for. He wanted to work with the people. This was the focus of his apostolate, but working with us gave that focus a wider context and prevented him from being one-sided. He was definitely searching at this period. I felt a great sense of social concern in him. His principal contribution to the group was his awareness of the presence of God in all this. It was easy just to be intellectual in these situations: Michael made us aware of God. The group was helped by Michael but it also helped him. A peculiar characteristic of his was that once he had an idea, he stuck to it and would not budge. On one occasion the whole group except Michael went out to dinner and on afterwards to a night club. When we told him about this later, he would not accept it and was not amused. There was no discussion: no attempt to persuade us that it was wrong for a group of Christian professional men to go to a night club, that it was an act of unfaithfulness to our wives, or set a bad example to others. He said none of this. It was simply that he did not understand how we could have done such a thing, even through weakness. He was an innocent.[19]

The lightness of his duties during his time at the chaplains' house gave Michael the opportunity to look around, observe and think about what he saw. It was, as Oscar Guarda had realised, a time of searching. Another of the groups which met regularly in the diocesan offices, were the Young Christian Workers. One member of this group later lived with Michael in Cerro Placeres. At this time he was studying electrical engineering at a technical college. He recalls how 'occasionally a very tall, friendly and cheerful newcomer, who had recently returned from France, would sit in on our meetings'. Michael did not become Chaplain to this group but was sufficiently impressed to think about introducing the Young Christian Workers to Peña Blanca when he moved there a couple of years later.[20] In the event he did not do so, but the YCW was to have an influence on his work with the Youth Group in the Parish.

A greater challenge to his thinking was provided by a rather different group whom Michael encountered in the Catholic University of Valparaiso. Luisa Celedon was a student in the Department of Social Work. The particular student group to which she belonged was different from and critical of the ordinary Catholic Action groups. Drawing members from various departments in the University, it preferred to remain outside the official structure of such groups by not having a chaplain and thus retaining its own independence. Its members believed that most of the official groups were unrealistic and saw the world through rose-tinted spectacles. This group wished to discuss how to be Christians in the real world. They had seen for themselves the hardships suffered by people living in the *poblaciones* on the hills above Valparaiso and wished to discuss the real problems of such people in practical terms, not just in theory. They were critical of traditional Catholic models of the role of women and did not want to have a priest chaplain because, owing to his seminary training, he would be unlikely to have his feet on the ground.

One day the group was settling down for a meeting in a room in the University when Michael came in. Luisa Celedon recognised him as someone she had seen around the campus attending student groups as a chaplain. The group leader asked him why he was there. She told him sharply that they had not decided to have a chaplain, let alone chosen who that would be. Michael replied that he was not there as a priest or as a chaplain. He was looking for a support group. They were suspicious that he might have been sent by the bishop to find out what was going on but felt unable to send him out in view of what he had said, even though they did not entirely believe him. So he stayed and listened and asked questions. In fact he ended up as a regular member of the group. His contributions and his personality came to be accepted and appreciated. Luisa Celedon remembered him as 'very young, fresh, with a positive if slightly naive view of things, extremely tall, very much a priest but a very good person, very friendly. He had strong faith and a great desire to be of help. He was always smiling'.[21] From the scant evidence of Michael's experience during this period, it is possible to detect something of the emerging rift in political attitudes among Chilean Catholics in the mid-sixties and to sense in which direction his own sympathies would develop.   1964 was the year when the term of office of the Chilean President, Jorge Alessandri came to an end and elections for a new President were to take place. Alessandri had been elected as an Independent in 1958 with the support of the Liberals and Conservatives. Primarily representing business interests, he hoped to create conditions for the private sector to develop the weak economy which he inherited. As an inducement to foreign capital there was a policy of state investment to prime the pump and of wage restraint to deter inflation. But though the domestic economy grew by 2.7% annually and unemployment fell from 9% to 5.5%, weak exports and increased foreign debt led to a balance of payments deficit, devaluation, and domestic inflation which by 1964 was running at about 50%. Government efforts to hold wages down led to a national strike and demonstrations, in November 1960, in which two workers were killed. Six more people were killed and many injured in protests and demonstrations after the 1962 devaluation. The Government gave in to the protests, thus accelerating inflation and affirming the new-found strength and confidence of the political Left.

Another reason for growing confidence on the political left in the early sixties was the example of the Cuban Revolution which claimed it was bringing education, health care and self-respect to its impoverished and neglected masses. Cuba stood as a beacon of hope to Marxist parties all over the Continent.

The three contestants in the 1964 elections were the official candidate of the Radicals, Liberals and Conservatives and heir presumptive to Alessandri, Julio Duran, the Christian Democrat leader, Eduardo Frei and the veteran Socialist candidate of the Popular Front, an alliance of Communists, Socialists and left wing Radicals, Salvador Allende. Allende had served as Health Minister in the Popular Front Government of Aguirre Cerda (1938-41) and had fought two Presidential elections already. In the 1958 election he had been less than three percentage points behind Alessandri.

The Christian Democrat Party only came into existence in 1957. Its origins were with a group of young Catholic members of the Conservative Party who, formed under Jesuit influence in the twenties and thirties on the social teaching of the Catholic Church, broke away from the Conservatives and formed the *Falange Nacional* in 1938. This new party gained credibility as a force for reform by its popular following in the growing rural labour movement in central Chile which, in November 1953, forced the Government of Carlos Ibanez to release its imprisoned leaders and pressure the landowners to negotiate with them. A second Conservative breakaway group, the Conservative Social Christian Party dissolved itself in 1957 and this encouraged most progressive Catholics along with former members of the Agrarian Labour Party to join forces in the new Christian Democrat Party in time to fight the 1958 election in which it polled 20.5% of the votes.

By 1964 Chilean politics were polarised by the spectre of Cuba and the fear of a Marxist electoral victory. Not only did the majority of the Chilean Right now join forces with the Christian Democrats under their leader Eduardo Frei, but the Party was vigorously supported by the Catholic Church and backed with funds and technical support by the various agencies of the United States Government, especially the Alliance for Progress and the Central Intelligence Agency. Frei campaigned on a platform of 'Revolution in Liberty'. For some it was a genuine attempt to bring about radical reform of Chilean society and a redistribution of wealth to benefit its poorer members. For others it was a shrewd or cynical move to stave off the greater evil of Allende. The result was a big majority of 56% for Frei. Allende polled 39% and Duran only 5%.[22] For the next six years, six out of the ten which Michael was to spend working in Chile, the country was ruled by a Christian Democrat Government.

NOTES

1. A major earthquake in 1906 virtually destroyed Valparaiso so these houses are doubtless of early twentieth-century construction.
2. Brian Loveman p.274 and David O.Toledo p.62.
3. Enrique Barilari 1992.
4. David O.Toledo pp.78-9.
5. *La Estrella*, 6th September 1968. The letter is anonymously signed *'Bikinista'*. Maruja Celedon, a devout Catholic living in Valparaiso, used

the beach referred to in the article for bathing in her bikini and also felt it necessary to go to Confession outside the diocese for fear of being questioned and excommunicated. (Conversation 1990).

6. Carlos Camus 1992.
7. David O.Toledo p.117.
8. Juan Jeanneret 1990.
9. Pepo Gutierrez 1990.
10. Joan Casanas 1997.
11. Alfredo Hudson 1990.
12. Eduardo Stangher 1990.
13. ibid.
14. ibid.
15. Carlos Camus 1992.
16. Alfredo Hudson 1990.
17. Enrique Barilari 1992.
18. The diocesan director was Pepo Gutierrez. He resigned from the post after the publication of *Humanae Vitae* in 1968.
19. Oscar Guarda 1992.
20. Willy Avaria 1995.
21. Luisa Celedon 1991. She was later elected Vice-President of the National Federation of Social Service Students (*Centro de Estudiantes de Servicio Social*) for all Chilean Universities.
22. For this historical resume I am indebted to Brian Loveman.

Michael with members of the Peña Blanca youth group in 1967

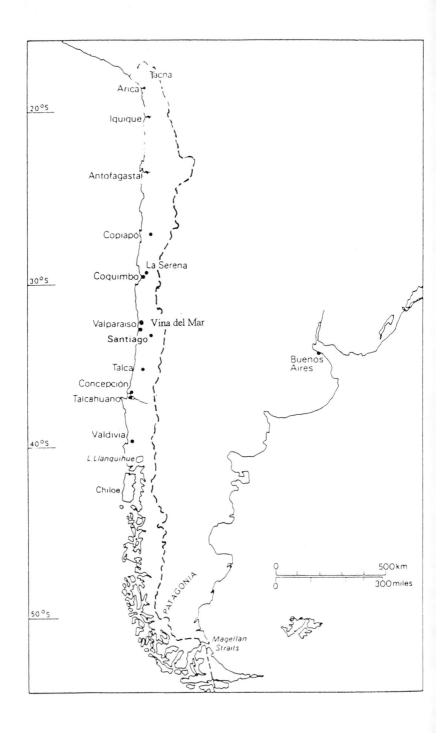

CHAPTER FOUR

PARISH PRIEST (1966-1970)

On the 11th June 1966, Michael was appointed priest in charge of the parish of Peña Blanca, a small town north east of Viña del Mar, about an hour by train and rather less by car from Valparaiso. Peña Blanca had no industry and served as a residential suburb for many of its largely middle class population who commuted to work. The parish buildings consisted of a large wooden church, since replaced, with presbytery and hall adjacent, the whole complex being enclosed by iron railings. It was probably the first time in his life that Michael had lived on his own. A widow in her sixties, Rosa Cerutti, acted as his housekeeper, but did not live in.

Peña Blanca was a watershed in Michael's life. He arrived with the intention of being an active, missionary-minded priest, visiting people where they lived or worked, being involved with groups and helping individuals to grow spiritually. To enable himself to do this effectively he bought a Vespa motor scooter. He rejected the model of the parish priest as a functionary, waiting at certain fixed hours in the parish office for the parishioners to come and consult him.[1]

Catechesis — the preparation of the young for the sacraments of penance or reconciliation, the eucharist and confirmation and of young adults for marriage and the baptism of their children — was a good place to start. With his training in Paris and his recent experience as a chaplain he was keen to be involved in the work himself.[2] He got to know the parish catechists and worked with them, accompanying them on visits to outlying country districts to give religious instruction to children and talk with their parents. It was a way of making contact with people and was, as he told his catechists, to be more than a matter of simply visiting their homes: they were to 'try and get close to the people, to find out from them the kinds of difficulties they were experiencing'.[3]

Religious education in local schools was another area in which Michael and his catechists were involved. The nearest secondary school was in the neighbouring town of Villa Alemana and soon after his arrival Michael started teaching there. One of the students was struck by the strange appearance of the new priest : over a clerical suit and Roman collar he wore a black leather jacket shorter than the suit jacket. When he came into the School he still had on his motor cycle helmet and leather gloves. The other feature which, not for the last time in Michael's life, attracted attention were his feet. For a man of his height they were probably a normal size, but to the eyes of a Chilean teenager, who was in any case small in comparison with his English or North American counterpart, they were gigantic. An extra-large, family bread-loaf called Monroy (*pan de Monroy*) featured frequently at that time on television commercials. Michael became known in the School as 'Monroy Feet' (*patas de Monroy*).[4]

Some students at the School had recently set up a Scout group on their own, without any help from adults. They held their meetings in a small hut and organised their own activities which included games, expeditions, and camps. One evening they were in the middle of a meeting when Michael, wearing helmet and gloves, appeared at the door. He asked about their activities and set-up, as if knowing nothing, though this, they later discovered, was not the case. Then, as if in response to their answers, he suggested that instead of using their cramped hut, they could, if they wished, clear out some vacant store rooms behind the presbytery in Peña Blanca which would provide more room and be a place of their own. The offer was accepted with alacrity and, before long, they had cleaned out, painted and installed electricity in their new meeting place. Michael did not attend their meetings but chatted with them afterwards, gradually getting to know them. He let them use a strip of land behind the house as a five-a-side football pitch and himself put up some netting on poles to stop the ball being kicked into the neighbours' gardens. The new rooms lacked running water, so the group were allowed to use the presbytery facilities. Such open-house informality on the part of a priest was unexpected.[5]

Whether because of the change in meeting place, however, or because at the age of sixteen or seventeen some of the members were growing out of it, the scout group declined in numbers. It is tempting to wonder if Michael himself weaned them away, his attitude to their scouting activities perhaps revealing his own lack of enthusiasm. His former headmaster, Dom Wilfrid Passmore, used frequently to ridicule scouting as an occupation for arrested adolescents, a jibe which Michael would not have forgotten. When eventually only the original eight members of the group remained, they decided to stay together, not as scouts but simply as friends and to continue meeting at the presbytery. This part of the process, at least, was gently moved along by Michael himself. As one of them put it: 'He guided us very subtly. He listened to our concerns and then, in conversation, suggested some possible courses of action. But he never imposed anything on us. That was what was so good about him: we never felt we were under his authority but that he was there with us'.[6]

Friends of the members and other young people from the parish came in to enlarge the group. By mid-1967, under Michael's influence, a new form of activity was emerging. They started in a modest way to help the residents of a *poblacion* on the outskirts of Villa Alemana by doing repairs and making improvements to their homes. These homes were for the most part wooden shacks with a single-pitch corrugated iron roof. The inside formed a single room for living, cooking, eating and sleeping, sometimes partitioned with plastic curtains for privacy. Michael acquired materials for the repairs from parishioners and learned the necessary techniques from local people. In one woman's home they repaired the roof and constructed a small outside kitchen. For others they built concrete walkways outside their houses so that they could avoid the mud in winter.[7] Michael and the group went out to the *poblacion* on Saturdays and sometimes on weekday afternoons. School finished at two. They met at the presbytery after lunching at their homes.

During the summer of 1967, the youth group made its first expedition away from Peña Blanca. Twelve of them went with Michael to Hierro Viejo, a mining village in the Andean foothills, lodging with the family of a seminarian whom Michael knew. The trip offered them a break from their home environment and an opportunity to get to know the local people. The villagers worked either in the local coal mines or on the land. The miners earned reasonable wages, much of which were spent in the bars. Many were alcoholics. The agricultural workers earned little. There was much poverty in the village. The group spent a week in Hierro Viejo, visiting homes, playing games and arranging sporting competitions for the children. At the end of the day they talked about their experiences. Michael would ask them what in particular had struck them and encouraged them to discuss any questions arising from this.

One of the better-off villagers had built himself a rough and ready swimming pool which he invited Michael's group to use. It was the first time they had seen Michael swimming and they were impressed by his skill. On that first occasion he appeared dressed as

Superman, in swimming trunks with a towel tied round his neck as a cloak and a big S sketched with coal on his chest. At the end of the week they organised a barbecue for the villagers. The food was followed by songs, stories, sketches and games. Michael also celebrated Mass a couple of times for them since there was no resident priest, but never put pressure on the group to attend. He simply let them know about it the night before and they were free to come or not as they wished. If they preferred to go to the swimming pool that was fine.

The following summer there was an expedition to Quintay, a small fishing village down the coast, south of Valparaiso. Finance for the youth group was a difficulty. On this trip they were subsidised by working with an organisation which ran summer camps for poor children. The youth group set up the children's camp at Quintay, pitching the tents, digging latrines, constructing makeshift kitchens. To carry equipment to the camp Michael had the use of a lorry on which he also loaded building materials for repairing some of the fishermen's homes.

The group spent the mornings working with the villagers to repair the wooden huts they lived in. They painted the outsides, decorated the interiors and constructed paths between the huts. The afternoons were free. On one of them they went out in a fishing boat. At the end of the week they invited the villagers to a barbecue at which they performed a song specially composed in their honour, a song about Chilean fishermen going out to sea. The Quintay villagers were touched by this attention. Michael himself, in the general euphoria, was persuaded to sing 'My bonny lies over the ocean', a first-time performance which he was made to repeat on many occasions. Mass was celebrated with the villagers in the Fishermen's Union social centre.

After the camp at Quintay the group, which until then had been male only, started to admit girls as members. The original group invited in friends and Michael asked some from the parish to join. Numbers rose to thirty or more. This development led eventually to several marriages between members. Michael, however, was concerned that individual relationships should not be an obstacle to group solidarity. At one time, when they were working over a series of week-ends in a new *poblacion*,[8] installing running water and helping to build a new primary school, there were as many as five couples among the group. They were surprised and a little upset when Michael insisted on their separation in the interests of group solidarity. He explained, first, that the girls' parents had let them come on the understanding that they would not be alone together; and second, that in his opinion they would very naturally pay more attention to each other and less to the group and its work. Friendship within the whole group was essential. Under Michael's influence there came to be an understanding among the boys that at *fiestas* no girl would ever be left on her own without invitations to dance.

Although suspicions, jealousies and conflict were to arise later, Michael took care to put the group members' parents in the picture. The original eight members had set up by their own initiative with Michael's encouragement. Nevertheless he soon made himself known to their parents, sometimes in a startling way. He made his first visit to the home of one member, whose father was in the Police and no friend of the Church, without any warning. He just appeared at the door in motor cycle helmet and gloves, saying 'I have come for a meal'. The member's mother was thrown into confusion because she had been brought up to believe that if the priest came, he should be entertained with proper ceremony and offered only the best food and wine. She had nothing special in the house. He saw she was embarrassed and said bluntly: 'If there's no food, I'll just have a cup of coffee with you. I have come to meet the family'. He became a friend of the household. The initially hostile policeman father, who treated his children in an authoritarian manner and expected to be addressed by them in the formal, old fashioned way, learned from Michael's example to dispense with the formal modes of address and be relaxed with his children.[9] Michael visited all the group members' families in similar fashion.

Members of the group had the freedom of the presbytery. They used its rooms for study and as a social centre. They collected together second-hand books of all kinds to serve as a library for their own use and the use of the parish. Though there were still occasional week-end expeditions to outlying *poblaciones,* regular meetings of the group now tended to be on Saturday evenings. At these meetings they usually took some theme for discussion in small groups followed by a general session at the end. Michael introduced the theme. The members had their own Bibles and Michael recommended certain texts to illuminate the topic. He would then come round to each of the groups and join in their discussions.[10] The themes were geared to the interests and experience of the members and included such topics as the nature of love and friendship. One of the members, a university graduate in Sociology[11] contributed to the Saturday meetings with talks on the sociology of friendship and companionship. Another member, a Geography student, spoke about stalactites. Some of the talks and discussions motivated the group for its work in the *poblaciones* which continued after the girls joined. They helped the women indoors with cooking and decorating; in one place they collected together unwanted books and magazines and formed a small library for the *poblacion*; the boys continued to do building repairs. After the day's work they all played games with the children.[12]

The group was not exclusive to Catholics: it was

open to those of other Christian denominations or none. Attempts were sometimes made to enter into political debate: it was difficult to avoid it in Chile at the best of times, and especially now that a Christian Democrat Government was attempting to bring about a socio-economic revolution in the country. One of the group was president of the Students' Union at his school and a paid-up member of the Radical Party, so from time to time a desire for political discussion was expressed. But the group came to the conclusion that it would cause divisions and so party political debate, at least, was avoided.

Political issues of a practical kind, however, were unavoidable on some of their expeditions, such as when they went, at the invitation of a Town Councillor to a village twelve kilometres from Pena Blanca called Los Molles. The people there were mainly agricultural labourers working on a large wine producing estate. The youth group had been invited to clear a piece of land and prepare it for a new school to be built. The work of cutting trees and scrub, digging out stumps, clearing and levelling the ground was hard and went on for several weekends. At Michael's suggestion they went into the homes of the villagers and got to know them. From these visits it became obvious that they suffered much hardship and deprivation. In conversation the group discovered that the workers were paid in the form of credits at a store belonging to and run by the owner of the estate. Attached to the store was a bar where the labourers could drink wine produced on the estate. This was also on credit. At the end of the month, with their drinking debts deducted from their wages, there was little credit left to buy food for their families. The food could only be bought at the store and was, in any case, overpriced.

One Saturday evening Michael and some of the group went into the bar. The labourers who were there drinking were surprised to see a priest come in. The estate owner was serving behind the bar. He was on his guard. Michael was invited to sit down by one of the men who had already had a fair amount to drink. The man filled up the single glass which was being passed round and offered it to him. Michael drained the glass, refilled it and handed it to the nearest of the group members who were with him. He got into a conversation with the estate workers about football, which teams would be the winners of the next day's matches. The owner asked him to celebrate Mass regularly on the estate. Next to his house and the estate office there was a chapel. He offered to pay for the Masses and to send a car to collect Michael and take him back to Peña Blanca each week end. Michael said that he was prepared to celebrate Mass if the workers or their families wanted it, but would do so in their sports centre because that was where the workers would feel more comfortable. He spoke separately to the men warning them to be on their guard against running up drinking bills and told the owner that the system was a form of exploitation. Whether anything changed as a result of their visit is doubtful.

The group discussed what they had observed in places like Los Molles and drew their own conclusions. Michael listened with interest, made his own comments, but never made comments which might encourage support for a particular political party. He was angry, however, when it became evident that the Town Councillor who had invited the group to Los Molles in the first place was using their work on the construction of the primary school as propaganda for the Christian Democrat party. Michael told him firmly that they were a Church group, not a political one, and that he had no right to use them to advance his own political campaign. The Councillor stopped supplying them with tools and materials and the work came to an end. In spite of the ban on party politics in the group this episode and their experiences in other *poblaciones* afforded them a considerable degree of political education.

The youth group was enlivened by social interaction of its own. There were informal gatherings when members brought food to share, Michael offered tea, one or two played the guitar and there was dancing and singing. On special occasions they held *fiestas* which included sketches and improvisations prepared beforehand. Such was the solidarity within the group that entertainments of this kind were easily set up. The seriousness of some of its activities was offset by a light-hearted side, especially in the earlier days when it was an all- male group. Perhaps Michael, in the absence of any more developed relationship, was re-living parts of his boarding school experience. Practical jokes were common: once the group set out on an early morning hike. Unnoticed by Michael, one of the members buried a large brick in the bottom of his rucksack. After some miles one of them suggested stopping for breakfast. 'Michael has a stone', he announced, 'on which to make the fire'. Michael was not amused. Another time, when they were relaxing on the beach at Quintay, some good-looking women were sunbathing a little distance away from them. Michael noticed the eyes of some of the group repeatedly turning in their direction. Wearing his swimming trunks he walked round and lay down between them and the women in a Marilyn Monroe posture. At home in the presbytery he was liable to fall victim to apple pie beds, tied up pyjama legs or sewn up trouser pockets. On their camps he retaliated by loosening the screws on their camp beds so that they collapsed when lain on. One of his party pieces was to tell a shaggy dog story about the Philistines which went on and on until they stopped him by giving him the bumps, tossing him ten times in the air on a blanket. As one of the girls put it, 'Fr Michael was the youngest of the group. He was the baby of them all, always laughing, always smiling, always happy'.[13]

The youth group was the most positive feature in Michael's time at Peña Blanca, though it is no surprise that it did not survive his departure by more than a couple of months. It provided companionship for him and gave him an opportunity to develop his own theological perspectives beyond the boundaries of formal religious practice. The young people, and the boys in particular, were free of what he came to call 'religiosity'. They were consequently open to a new understanding of what it meant to be a Christian in the world. They took part up to a point in parish social and liturgical life: 'Michael was very subtle: he brought us to the Church without our realising it', one of them said. But that was not really the point. All the signs are that Michael was not primarily interested in those who went regularly to church. He was instrumental in the opening of unbiased young minds and hearts to hear God's call to them to become real Christians in the real world, not in the formal, complacent structures of the Church. It was a process in which he was growing at the same time as the group. It was also a process which was dangerous.

Before the phrase was promulgated at Medellin in 1968, Michael had already made a preferential option for the poor, who came frequently to his door for help. He lived very simply himself and any money which was given to him he spent on clothes for people who could not afford them.[14] It was during his time at Peña Blanca that his father stopped sending him cheques as Christmas and birthday presents because he realised that the money would all be given away.[15] A couple he used to visit at this time said of him: 'He was the priest who was closest to people like us, people of modest means. We missed having such a priest when he left. The country people liked him very much. He inspired a great deal of trust'.[16] In his preaching he used Scripture quotations to emphasise

God's love for the poor. 'His homilies at Mass were always tender, spoken with love'.[17]

With those who were well off, however, he could be sharp. Peña Blanca had only one proper food store. The owner[18] was not a churchgoer, but his wife was devout and the family contributed to the parish finances. Without any local competition, prices at the store were thought to be excessive[19] although the owner's wife used to make up food parcels for poor families.[20] While Michael was in Peña Blanca the owner had a new store built and, when it was finished, asked Michael to bless it. Michael, however, refused to bless a shop 'which robbed the poor' and insisted that they should either charge lower prices or give ten per cent of their profits to the poor. The owner was enraged, complained to the bishop and called another priest in to perform the blessing. This was not the last time that Michael's attitude towards shopkeepers who, he believed, took excessive profits at the expense of poor people, was to arouse strong resentment.

The later sixties were a time of changes in the liturgy following the recent decrees of Vatican II. These changes caused upset in Peña Blanca as elsewhere in the Church. Michael was quick off the mark. He moved the altar from the east end of the church to the centre, placing the seats around it. Using the musical talents of the youth group, Peña Blanca was one of the first parishes in the diocese to start a folk Mass. Some parishioners were antagonised and moved away. But the church was thronged with young people.

The parish finances were another area of dispute. Michael refused to accept Mass stipends and made no attempt to raise money for the parish. He took no fees for baptisms, weddings and funerals from anyone who he considered could not afford them. As a result the finances were not healthy, the parish treasurer and Michael had a major row and, not surprisingly, the bishop was annoyed to receive an appeal for financial help.

Many of the long-standing parishioners were further antagonised by what seemed like the special privileges accorded to the youth group. Besides providing the music, members of the group did much of the reading at Sunday Masses. There was jealousy of their free access at all hours to the presbytery and parish rooms: some ladies of the parish campaigned to have this stopped. At least that was the way the youth group saw it.[21] Perhaps there was a reasonable desire by other groups to use the facilities and they clashed. Michael tried to bring peace but the conflict became embittered. A more serious accusation, made on more than one occasion to the bishop, was that the youth group engaged in politics, that the work they did in the *poblaciones* was politically motivated.

Complaints about Michael's moral teaching to the young also reached Bishop Tagle and caused him to express annoyance at Michael.[22] One of the teachings which upset him concerned the Sunday Mass obligation: If one went to Mass, Michael told them, it should be out of love, not from obligation. Another was that masturbation by adolescents is not a mortal sin.

The range of feeling towards Michael is revealed by a female member of the youth group:

> Fr Michael was very special for me. He became a kind of spiritual guide in my adolescence. He asked me to join a youth group in the parish. The next week-end I went and continued for about a year. There were around thirty-five of us in the group, of both sexes. Some were university students. I came to have a sincere friendship with Fr Michael. I can't remember whether I and the rest of the group called him by the familiar *tu* or not, but my impression is that he preferred it. On more than one occasion he spoke to me of certain inner doubts he had, doubts about his

vocation. In his talks to our group he would speak of relationships between men and women — later on several marriages came out of the group. He spoke of friendship, of 'going out' with a boy friend or girl friend and of sexuality. His teaching was important to me and I never found it shocking when he spoke about sex. I lived in Villa Alemana and did not normally come to Mass on Sundays in Peña Blanca, but I heard that he once spoke of sexuality in a homily and that some ladies in the congregation were offended and turned against him.

I didn't stay on in the group longer than a year because I let myself be influenced by certain people. These people did not like us going to the *fiestas*. And they disapproved of the social action our group was undertaking in the *poblacion*. I didn't know who all these people were but they were from Peña Blanca and included some of my relatives. Later on I rebelled against them and swore I would never join another youth group because it would not match up to Fr Michael's. I even heard - I don't know if it was true - that they got up a petition to have Fr Michael removed from Peña Blanca because they didn't like us having parties at the weekends, especially since there was wine at these parties. It was a surprise for me to discover that people did not like Fr Michael, that even some of our neighbours criticised him and that there was an attempt to get rid of him. In the end I was forbidden to go to the *poblaciones* with Fr Michael and the youth group. I was very angry and did not join any church group for the next twenty years as a result.[23]

Alejandro Belmar, who had been the leader of the original scout group, had the longest personal experience on which to base his assessment:

Michael took us out of the small world in which we lived, a very closed world, to all sorts of different places, places which were actually very close to us, all within our own Region. He showed us the world. He showed us Chile. We met workers, became aware that they all worked in different ways, and were all part of our own country which until then we hadn't known.

In Chile at that time there was a great desire for change, to change the way things were and make things better. I even think Michael may have been a little too hooked on this. A popular song of the time expressed the feeling very simply: It became a sort of hymn for us:

> *The world is changing*
> *And will change still more.*
> *The sky darkens*
> *Until it is ready to weep.*
> *The rain will fall*
> *But then will come clear sky at last.*[24]

Later, at University, I joined the Socialist Party. I needed to commit myself and it was a Christian commitment. Michael's role in this was fundamental. In later years I have not again felt Christ as I felt him at that time. Money, social position, all the things the world had to offer were of no importance. All that mattered was to serve the world and make it a better place. All that I learned from Michael.

Now that I am forty-five I can look back and see that the experience of the youth group was a good process, full of values which were not up in the air but to be found where we were, in our own lives. Michael grew with us. He did not just lead us: we led him too. It was reciprocal. Everything was talked through. Our group was a centre for Christian reflection. Michael simply provided us with a method.[25]

For the young man just quoted Michael was a friend, though one he looked up to and was influenced by. The female member of the group quoted earlier referred to the 'inner doubts' expressed by Michael himself. It was not just the antagonism of parishioners nor his impatience with the official, purely religious understanding of Christianity, but also a feeling of personal isolation, perhaps seldom expressed but of which he was increasingly aware, which gave rise to these doubts. During his time in Peña Blanca Michael began seeing his old seminary friend Patricio Guarda once a week in the *poblacion* on Cerro Placeres, above Valparaiso, where the latter now served as parish priest. The impression Patricio formed from these visits was that Michael experienced considerable loneliness and confusion. They may not have talked much about the youth group, but in relation to ordinary adult parishioners Patricio doubted that Michael ever spoke or understood their language fully. His limited communication with them was made more difficult since he was an intellectual who spent much time working with ideas. He organised the catechesis in the parish systematically, but with catechists who had been trained before his time. They never worked closely together. Patricio had a strong feeling of Michael's isolation: it was as if he lived in a castle.[26]

The conflict sparked off by the activities of the youth group in Peña Blanca mirrored a wider conflict involving young people in the diocese, as well as in other parts of Chile and all over the western world. The conflict in the diocese started in the Catholic University of Valparaiso. In June 1967, a deputation from the University of Valparaiso Students' Union approached the Chancellor of the University, who was none other than Bishop Emilio Tagle, proposing a series of democratic reforms to the University statutes and the removal of the of Rector whom they considered responsible for mismanagement of the finances. The bishop was not closed to the reforms in principle but insisted that they be considered by a Commission and then referred to the Holy See. He refused to remove the Rector. Later, when the

Rector was away in the Soviet Union attending a conference, the University Council voted to accept the proposed reform and to depose the Rector. Bishop Tagle, as Chancellor, vetoed the resolution and asked for the resignation of the Council. The students demonstrated and threw stones outside the diocesan offices. A new University Council was appointed. The students and some members of staff then occupied the University buildings for fifty-one days, the first of several such occupations of Chilean Universities.[27] The Ministry of Education mediated between the students and the Chancellor and eventually worked out a compromise. The reforms were mainly accepted. The Rector stayed in place until the end of his term. His successor was to be elected by students and staff. In the course of the dispute the students expressed their resentment in an attack on the role of the bishop: 'Only the intervention of the extra- academic authority (i.e.the bishop), which is not part of the University, but owing to the absurd feudal system in force controls its destiny, can prevent the reform'.[28] The origin of the University, opened with Catholic benefactions as recently as 1928, was now largely forgotten by the students or meant nothing to them. More importantly, in the course of the conflict Bishop Tagle became a symbol of outmoded opposition to the sixties' enthusiasm for change and renewal.

Not only university students but now clergy of the diocese came, through their desire for change, to find Bishop Tagle a stumbling-block to their aspirations. At about this time a number of priests who worked in *poblaciones* in the diocese grouped informally into what came to be known as the Mission to working people.[29] Many of them were non- Chileans and included most of the Spaniards and Catalans whom Tagle had drawn to Valparaiso. Perhaps because of his involvement in the *poblaciones* around Peña Blanca Michael was considered a member. The Mission group met from time to time to discuss common problems and, in the words of one of its members, 'gradually became aware of the gulf between where the people were and the demands made by the Diocesan Curia'.[30]

Most members of the Mission group, including Michael, joined the national movement of priests called Christians for Socialism.[31] When it started, this movement had eighty members. Increasingly disillusioned with what they saw as the failure of the Christian Democrat Government to bring about the revolution in Chilean society it had promised, they came to believe that the aims of a true Christian, that is to say the aims of a new and just society, were essentially socialist and that it was only by embracing Socialism that it was possible to be a genuine Christian in Chile at that time. Christians for Socialism later increased its membership to two hundred priests.

In September 1967, in the aftermath of the events in the Catholic University of Valparaiso, the Mission group called for the resignation of the two Vicars General of the Diocese[32] who, they claimed, were not in sympathy with their idea of how pastoral work should be conducted among the *poblaciones*. The two agreed with the bishop that for the sake of peace they would leave. They were replaced by a single Vicar General.[33]

Early the following year, 1968, there was a dispute with the bishop over the Mission group's support for reforms in the University of Santa Maria, another of Valparaiso's colleges of higher education. He severely admonished them for making a declaration of their support to a newspaper, *La Union*, which he succeeded in suppressing before it was published. In their reply to his official admonition, which they saw as an invitation to further dialogue between them, they said:

70

We believe this is the moment to tell you, Don Emilio, that we would like to see you beside us not only to admonish us when we make mistakes, but because we need your encouragement for whatever good we are able to contribute; we would like to see you more committed to the efforts of those who by your delegation are involved in our pastoral responsibilities; although we know the affection you have for us personally, in our pastoral work we feel you so out of reach, so removed from our concerns and from the people, that we find it difficult to realise that the *Presbiterium* to which we belong is one family with the bishop as its father.

Some months later, on the 11th August 1968, the Cathedral in Santiago was occupied for a few hours by a group of priests, nuns, students, trade unionists and the poets Angel and Isabel Parra. They demanded that the Church should redefine itself as defender of the oppressed and risk losing its own position of privilege by encouraging the liberation of those who are exploited. They were protesting at the consecration of the new Auxiliary Bishop. On the banner hoisted between the towers of the cathedral was written: 'For a Church alongside the People and its struggle'[34] The nationwide movement came to be known as the 'Church Alongside the People' or, more simply, the 'Church of the People'.

In Valparaiso the twenty-three priests of the Mission group decided that their dialogue with the bishop was getting nowhere. Their disagreement with him was made worse by the recent publication of *Humanae Vitae,* the papal encyclical forbidding artificial contraception, which Tagle interpreted more strictly than the other Chilean bishops. Above all they were conscious of the gulf between the daily experience of the people of the *poblaciones* and the current reality of the Church whose liturgy, hierarchy, laws and decision making were so remote from them. They lived with these people and wanted to see these people acknowledged and listened to as part of the Church. The twenty-three priests were meant to be working with and on behalf of the bishop in their parish communities, but they could not in conscience impose on their people the strict obedience to *Humanae Vitae* which he required. In view of their frustration at the remoteness of the bishop and official Church from the life of the working people, of which *Humanae Vitae* was but the latest example, they decided to resign from their parochial responsibilities. Some members of the group handed the resignation document personally to Tagle on the 15th August. At the same time there was a press statement by their spokesman, Dario Marcotti in which, among other things, he claimed that the Church had identified itself with the interests of the *bourgeoisie* and had modelled its own institutional apparatus on capitalist business enterprise.[35]

The bishop refused to accept the resignations,[36] but undertook a series of meetings with a standing committee from the group, the result of which was an agreed resolution expressing his confidence in the twenty-three priests in the exercise of their pastoral responsibilities, respecting their point of view, which it was hoped would be expressed and assimilated through the Diocesan Pastoral Council, and accepting, from 25th August, an elected representative of the twenty-three on to the Bishop's Council.

One of the twenty-three who signed the document of resignation was Michael. How closely he was involved with the group is uncertain. In no way was he one of the leaders. His poor communication skills in Spanish ensured that he never spoke or debated publicly on their behalf. He was, in any case, a man of deeds rather than words. He worked with the people of the *poblaciones* without making a lot of noise about it. It is doubtful that he took time off to attend many meetings. There is no record of his feelings towards Emilio Tagle, but it is unlikely that he expected personal support from him. Most probably he signed the resignation document because he agreed that the bishop and diocesan curia were out of touch with real life in the *poblaciones*, had a keen sense of the injustice their people suffered and of the Church's acquiescence in it, and finally because several of the signatories were his friends and he wished to be counted among them.

In April 1969, Michael was given permission to go on leave to Europe. An entry in the Valparaiso Diocesan archives, dated 25th April 1969, states that during his absence from Peña Blanca a new Priest-in-Charge is appointed with all lawful and customary faculties. It is not known how long his leave was for but, in view of the complaints he had received, the bishop may have been happy to extend it for as long as Michael wished.

Towards the end of April 1969, Michael took leave of his parish of Peña Blanca for a few months. Before he left, a memorable farewell party was organised by the youth group. It included a number of sketches in which Michael was portrayed as a massively tall and match-thin young man. Rosa, his housekeeper, who was also impersonated, expressed the hope that the replacement priest would be a small man so that there would be less trouser leg to iron. There was a cobbler and the inevitable jokes about Michael's feet. His parents, who greeted him on his arrival in Portugal were played by two diminutive teenagers. In Brazil, where he was stopping on his way, there were black dancing girls. Before the party ended there was a serious speech of thanks and a presentation.[37]

Michael spent some time with his parents in Estoril, whence they had retired from Brazil. His older sister Jocelyn and her husband Norman Henfrey were in

Estoril at the time and were amused that Michael was keen to acquire some photographic slides on marriage and sexuality for his youth group. They were puzzled that he had abandoned clerical dress altogether and did not reveal his identity to strangers. They thought he seemed 'a bit restless'. Michael himself was 'shocked' by how reactionary his father had become. Twenty five years before he had been progressive enough to introduce creches for the children of women employees of his company. He was also struck by the superficiality and luxurious lifestyle of his parents.[38]

He went on to visit his younger sister Pat and her husband Fred Bennetts in Madrid. Here he visited a tuberculosis sanatorium belonging to the Navy nearby and upset the authorities by asking the patients if they were receiving all the benefits and treatment they were entitled to. He celebrated Mass there but the Naval Chaplain would not let him preach, a prophetic brush with naval hostility to rocking the boat. During this holiday he was enthusiastic about a book he had been reading, Harvey Cox's *The Secular City*.[39]

Michael went on to do a short theological course in Paris. It was there that he received a visit from his Grange School and seminary companion Mariano Puga. Michael asked Mariano what he thought of his becoming a worker priest when he returned to Chile. Mariano replied that it was very important for the Church to enter fully into the life of working people. Michael said he intended to ask Don Emilio Tagle's permission to do this as soon as he got back.[40]

NOTES

1. Isabel Garcia 1990.
2. Hilda Arancibia 1990.
3. Maria Sagredo 1990.

4. Mario Abarsua 1992.
5. ibid.
6. ibid.
7. 'Fr Michael used to go and help the poor people out on the hills. I remember seeing him pushing a wheelbarrow full of tiles'. (Hilda de Arancibia 1990). 8. At Cuesta de la Dormida
9. Mario Abarsua 1992.
10. Cecilia Curiapil 1990.
11. Lautaro Prado.
12. Cecilia Curiapil 1990.
13. ibid.
14. Matilda Silva 1990.
15. Pat Bennetts 1990.
16. Raul and Marisol Pimentel de Soto 1990.
17. ibid.
18. Santiago Cuneo.
19. Maria Sagredo 1990.
20. Hilda Arancibia.
21. According to Mario Abarsua.
22. Mafalda Benvenuto 1990.
23. Cecilia Curiapil 1990.
24. *El mundo esta cambiando y cambiara mas.*
   El cielo se esta nublando hasta ponerse a llorar.
   Y la lluvia caera
   Luego vendra el sereno.
25. Alejandro Belmar 1992.
26. Patricio Garda 1991.
27. Sources: a) Conversation with Fr Wenceslao Barra 1990. Barra was the bishop's representative on the University Council but agreed with the students' proposals. He therefore abstained in the vote and subsequently resigned. Later in the same year he was invited by Archbishop Silva Henriquez to move to the Diocese of Santiago. He did not return until after Tagle's retirement twenty years later. b) David O.Toledo pp.96-7
28. David O.Toledo. ibid.
29. *Equipo de Pastoral Obrera.*
30. Pepo Gutiérrez 1992.

A more critical appraisal is offered by another contemporary who was not a member of the group: 'They were critical of everything ... anarchical. The Catalans had a great influence in all that: they were tremendous anarchists. They were critical of the Young Christian Worker movement in which we were working with enthusiasm and hope, critical of Catholic Action, critical of the structures of the Church, highly critical of the Christian Democrats who were doing all they could to bring about social change. They tore everything to bits. They were very nice people. We had many laughs together. It would have been tremendous if.... Don

Emilio was very fond of them and gave them a lot of support. When he realised what was happening it was too late'. (Carlos Camus 1992).

31. *Cristianos por el Socialismo*. Founded in Santiago by Gonzalo Arroyo SJ.

32. Wenceslao Barra and Enrique Barilari.

33. Carlos Zita who resigned two years later and was replaced by Jorge Bosagna.

34. *Por una Iglesia junto al Pueblo y su Lucha*.

35. Dario Marcotti was a parish priest on one of the *cerros* who earned his living as a carpenter nearby. He had been a member of the Chilean Communist Party since his return from Paris a few years before. Asked in an interview in the Valparaiso evening paper, *La Estrella*, (Sept 7, 1968) whether he believed in God, Marcotti replied: 'He is the Father of all without distinction'. And Mary? 'A brave, decisive and simple woman like one of our working class mums (*como las mamas de nuestro pueblo*)'. Asked what he thought of Camilo Torres, Marcotti said: 'An outstanding man who gave great hope to the people of Latin America who saw the Church far away from them and now see it closer'.

36. According to Pepo Gutiérrez the twenty-three resigned in the hope that pressure would bring the bishop to his senses. They did not expect or want to be suspended from the priesthood. (Pepo Gutiérrez 1992).

37. The speech was made by Lautaro Prado. (Mario Abarsua 1992).

38. Pat Bennetts 1990.

39. ibid.

40. Mariano Puga 1990. Mariano conjectures that the bishop refused but that Michael went ahead nevertheless.

CHAPTER FIVE

CHANGING WORLDS (1969-1971)

In 1964, when Michael was at the Chaplains' house in Valparaiso, his seminary friend, Patricio Guarda, had gone to live and work as parish priest in a new urban development on Cerro Placeres, the northernmost hill (*cerro*) of the port city. The development, built with German money, was called Villa Berlin. The bottom part of Cerro Placeres was of early twentieth-century construction and had an established parish church of its own. In the 1960's country people migrating to the city settled further and further up this and all the other hills behind the Valparaiso seaboard. It was to a couple of parish Christian communities among the new settlements up the hill that Patricio was to be the priest.[1] A year after his arrival, four religious sisters[2] came from Namur in Belgium to help him with the pastoral work. In due course they moved into a house built for them next to the new chapel of St Barbara. Patricio himself had a modest wooden house built a short distance away.

By this time Michael was in Peña Blanca. Patricio was not only an old friend but living and working in a *milieu* towards which Michael was increasingly drawn — the working-class world of the *poblacion*. He developed the habit of going over every week on his motor bike to Cerro Placeres to meet up with Patricio. The latter at first thought that he could help Michael, but soon found that the support was mutual:

> We were each seeking our own way forward. I was conservative. He felt tied down by the formalities of being a parish priest. He saw what I was doing and he saw what he wanted to do. One day he simply decided to leave Peña Blanca and come and live in my house. He never wanted

to get involved in my pastoral work. He made friends with my friends but he sought his own way. This was to be a priest worker. He didn't want privilege. My profession as parish priest was privileged. He wanted to be a man like others who had to earn his own living. This was to be his witness to the Gospel. He wanted to experience the same circumstances and living conditions as the poor, working with them in an industrial enterprise which used them to its own advantage.[3]

At the end of the European summer, probably in early September 1969, Michael had returned to Peña Blanca from his parents' home in Portugal. He continued in the parish for a couple of months while looking for an opportunity to implement the decision he had made with Mariano Puga in Paris — the decision to abandon the middle-class environment in which he had been brought up, including the clerical environment of church and presbytery, and to take up the new life of an industrial worker. It was probably only when he had found a practical way of entering into the world of industry, had in fact been offered a job, that he finally abandoned Peña Blanca, its parish duties, its conflicts and the youth group whose members were in any case growing up and moving away. There is no evidence in the diocesan archives of any arrangement with the ecclesiastical authorities for him to leave: probably it was presented to them as a *fait accompli*.[4]

The move to Cerro Placeres towards the end of 1969 was the most decisive and dramatic step Michael took in his life, more significant even than his return to Chile to become a priest, from which it stemmed. In taking it, he crossed a boundary from which there could be no turning back. To ease his transition he joined his friend Patricio Guarda for the time being in Villa Berlin. The sanctuary Patricio provided served as a half-way house between two worlds, a base camp from which to make the final ascent.

It was not Michael's intention to continue as a professional member of the clergy from day to day, but in his new surroundings he celebrated Mass with Patricio and the Sisters in the chapel of Saint Barbara, standing in on occasional Sundays when Patricio was away. He attended the area's neighbourhood Council meetings at which Patricio presided. A local resident remembers that Michael was astute in assisting those who needed to acquire title deeds to the land on which they built their homes, something he had learned in his dealings with residents of the new *poblaciones* around Peña Blanca.[5] All the land on Cerro Placeres was privately owned and those who came and established themselves there bought a plot from a previous owner. If the plot was subsequently resold without the previous purchase having been entered into the land register in Valparaiso, the new householder could forfeit his property.

Shortly after Michael's arrival, he and Patricio were joined by a young man, prominent in the Young Christian Worker movement, whom they had both known during their time as student chaplains: Willy Avaria, subsequently an active Party member of the Christian Democrats, who later still was involved in the setting up of the breakaway Party, *MAPU*, went to live with them and work as a kind of pastoral assistant to Patricio.[6] Michael turned his attention to a new area, further up the hill, where people were migrating from the country in a steady stream and setting up their own dwellings. This area was now given the name Poblacion Progreso. Here he in his turn worked to form a Christian community, celebrating Mass with them in a neighbourhood community centre.

Michael had come to Cerro Placeres, however, with the intention of becoming a worker priest and, from the moment he arrived there, he set about implementing his intention. A *Curriculum Vitae* addressed to the Institute for Professional Qualification[7] dated 29th September 1969, shows that very soon after his return from Europe he was seeking recognition of his London University Engineering degree as a qualification for a skilled industrial job. How long it took him and what job possibilities he explored is not known but on 3rd December 1969, he received his first wage packet from the shipyard of Las Habas. Wages were normally paid at the end of the month so it is reasonable to assume that Michael started work there sometime during the month of November.

Las Habas was situated at the opposite end of Valparaiso from Cerro Placeres, beyond the harbour and the old town in an area called Playa Ancha. As a shipyard it specialised in repairs rather than shipbuilding, had a smelting plant where all metal components were manufactured and repaired, and a floating dry dock for work on the hull. In the sixties the yard employed at least six hundred workers and was, since its workforce was unionised and belonged to various political parties, a place of constant and heated debate.

The shipyard operated on a shift system, the shifts being from six in the morning till two in the afternoon, from two till ten at night and from ten till six in the morning. Michael worked the morning shift which meant leaving home around 5am. He operated a lathe, making propellers, axles and other parts needed for the ship repairs. It was specialised and highly skilled work, at times also hot and gruelling. His hands were exposed to frequent minor but painful injuries. A parishioner from Peña Blanca, who had given guitar lessons to members of the youth group, encountered him one day in 1970 in a bus in Valparaiso. 'He showed me his hands. They were bruised and scarred all over'.[8] A septic finger which caused him much pain, and then embarrassment when he needed to receive an anti-biotic injection in his bottom, administered by Patricio, was the consequence of one of these injuries at work.

Michael used to come home to Patricio's house in the afternoon worn out, but he recounted his experiences in the shipyard with enthusiasm. There were no more problems about sleeping. He was in bed and asleep by nine in the evening, ready for the early start next morning.[9] When Mariano Puga returned to Chile from France he went as soon as he could to visit Michael in the shipyard. On arriving there, he asked for 'Maestro Woodward'. They said: 'The Gringo?' Eventually Michael himself appeared wearing a hard hat and overalls 'looking worn out'.[10]

Michael's cheerfulness was not dented by the coarse treatment to which he was subjected in his early days at the yard. To the other workers the appearance of a very tall, gaunt European, dressed in overalls, working at a lathe, caused a sensation. He was the topic of much discussion and speculation, even though they did not know at first that he was a priest. Initially they suspected him of being on an ego trip, planting himself in these alien surroundings as some kind of heroic gesture. They wanted to discover how genuine he was in choosing to work with them, just how truly he desired to be one of them. They recognised his background and culture as far removed from their own and, unable to read him for that reason, they set about in their own way working out what he was up to. Their method was not characterised by hostility so much as by their own brand of humour. They played simple practical jokes on him, such as hiding his shoes. Workers had to change on entering and leaving the shipyard and Michael's shoes were noticed, as they had been at Peña Blanca, for their ample dimensions. After the day's work he went to change into his ordinary clothes before leaving and could not find his shoes. Having searched everywhere amid the taunting of the other workers, he eventually caught sight of them dangling from the top of a high crane. There were other jokes of a coarser character.

Michael's courtesy and good manners were initially a challenge to his fellow workers and something of a barrier between them. For their part they regarded it as a virtue to be both down-to-earth and *macho* in their use of language which was, as a result, colourful in sexual imagery, if limited in range. They deliberately exaggerated this aspect in any conversation with him. Las Habas was close to the port area of Valparaiso whose streets were full of brothels.[11] It was normal for some of the men at the shipyard, on receiving their wage packet at the end of the month, to pay these a visit. In his early days there they put pressure on Michael to join them on these sorties, telling him that, if he really wanted to prove that he was one of them, this was the way to do it. The outcome of the prolonged assessment by his workmates was evidently not impaired by his refusal.

It did not take very long, in fact, for the other workers at the yard to be convinced that Michael was indeed genuine, in spite of his strange appearance and manner. It became known, too, that he was a priest. That in itself would not have been enough, but coupled with his transparent honesty and simplicity, it was an invitation for them to seek him out with their problems and confide in him. For that is what happened. He took on a pastoral role. His advice was increasingly sought. When given, it was, according to one worker, always balanced and received appreciatively.[12] Besides acting as unofficial counsellor, whenever it was possible, he offered practical help. On one occasion he took a workmate back to Cerro Placeres. The man had a wife and baby but no home. With the help of some friends Michael succeeded in acquiring a basic dwelling place which housed the family for several years.[13]

Politically Michael was known to share the views of what was coming to be known as the Theology of

Liberation, but he showed no signs to the other workers of being an adherent of any political party. In spite of all the debate which took place in the shipyard — Salvador Allende, the future President of the Republic, paid it a visit early in his 1970 electoral campaign — Michael appeared to be above party differences.[14] In his final months at Las Habas, towards the end of 1970, when the new Government was in power, he was elected by his fellow-workers to the committee on which workers and management discussed working conditions, especially matters of health and safety. He took a particular interest in the provision of educational opportunities for the workforce, an area into which he was himself soon to move. In the following year Las Habas was taken into state ownership and Michael's committee was involved in an early stage of discussions leading to that.[15]

At home in Cerro Placeres, until the end of 1970, Michael had the companionship of Patricio and Willy, with the Dominican Sisters living nearby. By virtue of their common background and long acquaintance, Patricio was the person closest to him though it was not an emotional closeness. Warm relations existed between Michael and some parishioners in the *poblacion,* relations which afforded him a degree of vicarious domesticity which he otherwise lacked. Victor Bernal and his wife Norma, members of the Christian community of Saint Barbara, made Michael welcome in their home nearby and he got into the habit of visiting them on Monday afternoons after his return from Las Habas. He usually brought food for the meal: eggs, tinned sausages, and sometimes a few bananas were his customary contribution. Norma cooked these, adding bread and other items and generally made tea for them all. After eating they stayed quiet for a moment at the table in prayer. Michael claimed that whatever he prayed for with them was fulfilled. Norma fetched a Bible and they read a passage from the Gospels, especially Matthew or Luke. After reflecting silently on the passage, each of them articulated their own understanding of it. Michael explained whatever they found obscure or difficult, often correcting their interpretations. They read these gospel passages in the light of their experience of life in their neighbourhood. They particularly tried to read them through the eyes of those of their neighbours who were hardest up or destitute. Michael taught them to see Christianity not as a religion but as a personal way of living. Anything else was mere religiosity. A favourite text which he often used for prayer and meditation, was Psalm 92:

It is good to give thanks to the Lord,
to sing praises to your name, O most High;
to declare your steadfast love in the morning,
and your faithfulness by night,

For you, O Lord, have made me glad by your work;
at the work of your hands I sing for joy.
How great are your works, O Lord!
Your thoughts are very deep!

The dull man cannot know,
the stupid man cannot understand this:
that, though the wicked sprout like grass
and all evil-doers flourish,
they are doomed to destruction for ever...

The righteous flourish like the palm tree,
and grow like a cedar in Lebanon.
They flourish in the courts of our God.

They still bring forth fruit in old age,
they are ever full of sap and green,
to show that the Lord is upright;

he is my rock, and there is no unrighteousness in him.

Rejoicing at the works of God's hands led to a meditation on the daily work of a household, especially on the preparation of food. If this was at times a tedious chore, it was right to do it gladly, to be grateful for the 'work of God's hands' of which they were making use, to think of those who had planted and harvested it and caused it to grow. Being full of sap and green was an important image: God's sap flowed in those who kept their heart pure. For such people there was no growing old.[16]

As early as October 1969, before he started working at Las Habas, and possibly even before he had left Peña Blanca, Michael paid a deposit [17] on a plot of land in the new Poblacion Progreso, the area a kilometre further up the hill from Villa Berlin where he had been visiting newly settled families and inviting them to join a new Christian community.[18] Poblacion Progreso was not, like Villa Berlin, built with foreign aid, but each of the shanty dwellings was set up by the new settlers themselves. Over the years wooden shacks gave way to more solid, but still rudimentary, single storey houses of adobe or breeze blocks with roofs of corrugated iron. On 6th April 1970, Michael completed his payment to a government housing agency for the purchase of a prefabricated *mediagua,* the cheapest form of housing available.[19] His plot of land was on the corner of a new mud road called, somewhat improbably, Buenos Aires Street. The prefab was erected at the front of the plot leaving room behind for the house which Michael intended to build for himself. The ground at the back of the plot fell steeply away into a gully. Michael did not leave Patricio's house immediately. The prefab was to have other occupants.

Sometime in the first few months of 1970 three post-graduate Philosophy students in the Catholic University made the decision to go and live together in one of the new *poblaciones* which were springing up around the edges of the city. One of them, Lautaro Prado, had been connected with the youth group and known Michael well in Peña Blanca. He had made the farewell speech in his honour at Michael's leaving party. Lautaro told his student friends about the enthusiastic, forward looking, young priest who used to visit Cerro Placeres every week and was unhappy in the middle-class environment of Peña Blanca. So he and his two friends, Manuel Rojas and Jaime Contreras, made contact with Michael in Villa Berlin. They had already formulated their aims: they wanted 'to live a Christian life, to live with and help the poor, to be involved in their political struggle'.

The three young men had been members of a student Catholic Action group in the University led by one of the Catalan priests. Members of this group regularly did voluntary work on welfare projects run by the Students' Union. Lautaro, Manuel and Jaime had helped on several summer camps for young people from the *poblaciones*. In February 1970, they organised one themselves for poor children from the town of Quillota.[20] The programme included reflection and discussion on contemporary Chile, carried out in the company of some of the inhabitants of the village where the camp was held, manual work out of doors in the afternoons and in the evenings there were camp fires and barbecues.

The success of their summer camp was a major factor in the decision of the three young men to join Michael in Cerro Placeres. The erection of the prefab in Buenos Aires Street determined the timing of their arrival — June 1970. Michael and the priest who had gathered poor children from Quillota for their summer camp, helped Manuel and Jaime move their belongings from their parental homes, though there was little room in their new home. Meanwhile Michael, with his Civil Engineering degree from King's College, London, behind him and with some help from an architect cousin who lived in Viña, drew up plans for the house to be built behind the prefab.[21] Work started and took place mainly at weekends, when Michael was at home. The students helped when they had time. It took about a year to complete.

A neighbour living across the road, cooked their evening meal for them. Sometimes Michael obtained bread and wine from her to celebrate Mass in the prefab. The three students, Michael and sometimes a neighbour would be present. As one of the young men described it:

> Michael did not 'say' Mass. We all joined in on equal terms, except for the consecration itself. We did it sitting round the living room table. Each of us commented on the Scripture readings. Michael did not use any printed texts for the rest of the Mass but prayed in his own words with calm and recollection. The words came from within and were said with great faith. There was never a trace of doubt in his words and I think that he never doubted his basic religious convictions.[22]

1970 in Chile was a year of presidential elections. The Christian Democrats were considered by the political Right to have been excessively radical in their agrarian reform programme. By the Left and by many Christian Democrats themselves they were thought to have failed in their attempt to bring about a 'revolution in liberty'. This time the electorate was offered three choices. The former President Jorge Alessandri was presented by the Right as a senior and respected candidate on an Independent ticket. The Christian Democrats promised to continue and complete their revolution under the more radical leadership of Radomiro Tomic. The parties of the Left united once again under the leadership of the veteran Salvador Allende, candidate of the *Unidad Popular*.

The elections took place on the 4th September.

Allende and the *Unidad Popular* led the poll by the narrow margin of 36.3% over Alessandri and the Radicals with 35%. These were followed by Tomic and the Christian Democrats with 27.8%. It was a decisive moment in Chilean history. A Marxist Government had been democratically elected during the Cold War in a country belonging to the 'free' world. For seven weeks it was touch and go whether Allende's election would be ratified by the Chilean Congress. President Nixon ordered the Central Intelligence Agency to do all it could to prevent ratification. The Chilean business community was in a panic.

A few days after the elections, on the 9th September, eighteen priests of the Working People's Mission group in Valparaiso, of whom Michael was one, signed a declaration of support:

> A few days after the presidential elections we are deeply concerned that so many people, among whom many self-proclaimed Christians, are putting their own interests before the common good of the whole of Chile. They are ready to reduce the country to chaos rather than cooperate with a Government which frightens them because it may limit their wealth or privileges.
>
> What purpose does it serve to mention developments which all know about: flight of capital, departures from the country, economic boycotts, etc? We recall the words of the Gospel, how difficult it is for a rich man to enter the Kingdom of Heaven, that we are called to detachment, service and disinterested self-giving to the common good.
>
> We wish for the 'miracle' of a better Chile. As in the Gospel account of the multiplication of the loaves and fishes, people are needed today with the trust of that boy who was prepared to hand over his bread and his fish so that the miracle could be worked.
>
> Beyond all fear there is a duty for Christians and people of goodwill to cooperate even at the cost of personal sacrifices with the process which the country has freely

chosen for the construction of a more just society, knowing for certain that God is also involved in this task.

Two days before the Congress vote, the Commander in Chief of the Armed Forces, General Schneider, a supporter of the constitutional way forward, was gunned down and fatally wounded in a bungled attempt by members of the right wing group, *Patria y Libertad*, to 'kidnap' him and cause a breakdown in law and order which would sway Congress against ratification. But on the 24th October Allende was ratified by an overwhelming majority in Congress, having given assurances to the Christian Democrats that democratic freedoms would not be abolished. The Christian Democrat leader Radomiro Tomic went personally to Allende's house to congratulate him. He was inaugurated as President on 3rd November, starting his time as Comrade President with great popular support. It was the least he needed if his ambitious plan to revolutionise Chilean society by giving economic and political power to the workers was to come anywhere near fruition. By itself popular support was not enough.[23]

A major change also occurred in Michael's life at the end of 1970. In December Patricio, having obtained a dispensation from Rome to leave the priesthood, was married to Marie-Claire, one of the sisters in Villa Berlin. The wedding took place in Cerro Placeres. Michael and one of the Catalan priests concelebrated the Nuptial Mass. Michael was idealistic about the wedding and happy for the couple. He had a large poster with the words 'God is Love' placed above the altar. Patricio and Marie-Claire left Cerro Placeres after the wedding and settled in Concepcion in the south of Chile.[24] There is no evidence of Michael's deeper feelings at this point but it is hard to avoid the conclusion that, with Patricio's departure, a significant link with his past, most particularly with memories of the Seminary and what that meant for his priestly identity, was severed. From now on there was less to hold him in the long run to that celibate identity. But for a man of his integrity the only alternative to celibacy was a fully committed marriage. In the meantime the cravings of loneliness were kept at bay by an active concern for others.

With the changes in the country brought about by the election of the new Government and the change in Michael's life caused by Patricio's departure, there now came an additional upheaval of his own choice. He was offered a post in the Centre for Studies and Industrial Training, a department of the Catholic University of Valparaiso known as *CESCLA*, its Spanish acronym.[25] He was in some doubt as to whether he should accept the offer. By now he was happy working at Las Habas and had gained the respect of his workmates. On the other hand *CESCLA* would give him influence over a larger section of the industrial world. His fourteen months' experience as a skilled industrial worker would be a considerable asset in a broader teaching post where he would know at first hand what his worker students were going through. He accepted the appointment and, in February 1971, began to work in his new post.[26]

CESCLA was a sort of workers' university. Its aim was to enable industrial workers to gain a university qualification. It achieved this in two stages: first by bringing workers who wanted it through primary and secondary levels of general education; secondly by training those who had reached this level to become qualified in technical engineering skills. The teaching during the first stage was related as closely as possible to the students' previous work experience. The second phase involved a four year university course and included mechanical, electrical, electronic and civil engineering.

CESCLA itself taught the pre-university qualifying courses only. The *CESCLA* students on the second phase were taught in the appropriate university department.

Phase one lasted two years with a hundred and fifty students in each year. When the operation was in full swing, the Catholic University of Valparaiso had eight hundred *CESCLA* students. They came from the industrial sector from all over the Fifth Region of Chile and included railway and gas company workers, workers from the Port of Valparaiso and the Las Habas repair yard, from factories and industrial works of all kinds. *CESCLA* was not an invention of the *Unidad Popular* but had been set up under the Christian Democrat Government as part of its programme to improve the skills and qualifications of low-paid manual workers. The new Government strengthened and extended its work, providing generous financial resources. It was the first department of the University to be closed after the military Coup in 1973. By then the first batch of students had graduated.[27]

As his first assignment for *CESCLA*, in February 1971, Michael helped to run a 'summer university'[28] for workers from the industrial towns of Quillota and Calera. University staff and students spent a month of their summer vacation providing talks and seminars, films and plays for factory and agricultural workers, *poblacion* dwellers, women and young people. This particular session was inaugurated by President Allende himself. The following month he took up his role as teacher of secondary level Physics and Maths. Classes took place from six in the evening until ten, but Michael worked a full forty-hour week, the rest of the time being taken up with administration and planning. From early 1972 he was going out two days a week to Calera where *CESCLA* had an out-station. A young Physics graduate[29] worked as Michael's assistant. They planned the classes together, trying always to gain the students' interest and motivation by referring to their own practical experience. The Physics course was also partly historical, relating how knowledge and technology had developed up to the present.[30]

The three students who had come to join him on Cerro Placeres influenced Michael in another important step he took in early 1971. During this period Chile must have been the most highly politicized country in the world. The debates which were a daily occurrence in the shipyard of Las Habas were occurring all over the country. With the accession of Allende to power they increased further and, throughout its three years, became ever more intense. The three Philosophy students who came to Placeres had moved towards political involvement in their time as members of student Catholic Action when they took part in the summer camps for disadvantaged children. Simple awareness of the vast inequalities in Chilean society and, in particular, the plight of its poorest and weakest members, had this effect on any fair-minded young person with energy to spare. Political involvement was encouraged by Catholic Action which at first put its weight behind the Christian Democrat Party, but the latter's five years in Government had failed to satisfy those who were impatient for justice. Many of its supporters now moved further to the political left.

The question of which party to join was exercising Lautaro, Jaime and Manuel on their summer camp in February 1970. Rodrigo Gonzalez, the Philosophy lecturer who had instigated the camp, was a prominent member of *MAPU*.[31] Fr Antonio Llido, with whom they worked on the camp and became friendly, hoped they would join the more extreme *MIR*,[32] of which he was himself a member. A social work student[33] who helped run the camp and later became Lautaro's wife, was already a member of *MAPU*. Whether that was an influence or not, it was for *MAPU* that they eventually opted.

The Unified Movement for Political Action (*MAPU*) was brought into existence in May 1969 by a group of young people, intellectuals, agricultural and industrial workers who had broken off the year before from the Christian Democrat Party because of what they saw as the failure of Eduardo Frei to implement his promised reforms. *MAPU* aimed to be a third force within the Left, between Socialism and Communism. It hoped to bring the two rivals into one unified party of the Left and to put an end to electoral competition between them. At its first party conference in 1969 it defined itself as Marxist-Leninist. A faction of the new Party itself broke away after this first conference because it did not wish to be Marxist. It called itself the Christian Left. *MAPU* was a Christian party: many former members of Catholic Action groups joined it. It had a particular appeal to intellectuals, hence its strength among teachers and university lecturers. It placed much emphasis on the role of education in socio-economic reform, being influenced by Pablo Freire's ideas on empowering working people to change their situation for themselves by educating them to understand its social, legal and political possibilities.

In 1970 *MAPU* became part of the *Unidad Popular* coalition before Allende's election campaign and took part in the new Government. It considered itself a revolutionary party in the Latin American tradition, fostering the development of popular power. Its own decisions were always to be reached democratically. In support of its goal of social justice, it was prepared to countenance all forms of struggle, including, if necessary, the use of armed force – something a few of its followers later resorted to in response to the violence of the Coup.

CESCLA, though founded earlier, thoroughly embodied the aims and ideals of *MAPU*. *CESCLA*'s head, Rodrigo Gonzalez, and nearly all its staff were *MAPU* members. The evidence suggests that Michael had not joined *MAPU* before he left Las Habas at the end of 1970, but the example of Lautaro, Jaime and Manuel together with the prevailing ethos of *CESCLA,* of which he was now to be a part, may have put pressure on him to join *MAPU* himself. It seems to have provoked something of a struggle of conscience.

One day at the beginning of 1971, when he was involved in the summer University, Michael got into conversation with a fellow-passenger on the bus going to Calera. Myrta Crocco, was a lecturer in the department of Social Work in the Catholic University. They spoke about the Catholic Church in Chile, about the occupation of Santiago Cathedral in August 1968 and of a recent meeting of about sixty people in the Catholic University of Valparaiso who also accused the Church of a lack of concern for the disadvantaged members of society. This led on to a discussion of the crisis of Christianity: how could they reconcile the Gospel with church authorities who always supported the bosses? All the rules, structures and order became a nonsense for someone living and working in the world of the *poblaciones.* Michael told Myrta that he had been working recently in the ship repair yard of Las Habas and that he was living alone on Cerro Placeres: he was concerned as to whether or not he should become an active member of a political party. It was clear to Myrta that his inspiration was Christian: he saw it as his Christian duty to be where he was in the *poblacion.* In her words, 'he slept badly, ate badly and was cut off from contact with people of his own culture. But he had great strength'.[34]

Later in the year, probably after he had become a member of *MAPU*, Michael discussed the question of belonging to a political party as a priest with his old friend from seminary, Pepo Gutíerrez. They met in the University where Pepo was a lecturer in the Theology department and Michael was already working in *CESCLA*. As Pepo recalls the discussion, Michael was convinced that the only way to change society according to gospel

94

values was through some kind of political grouping, such as a political party, a trade union or a local neighbourhood council. You could not achieve much on your own. At a time when virtually everyone around him was a member of a political party, he had lacked a means of channelling his desire to work for change. To be effective such work needed structure and organisation, not endless meetings, which Michael disliked. He and Pepo saw the issue from different standpoints. Pepo had a platform in the University from which, as a highly articulate lecturer, he was able to influence a fair number of students. Michael, who was, in any case, more of a doer than a talker, saw himself, in spite of his *CESCLA* work, as involved primarily where he lived, in the *poblacion.* To have an impact in such a context it was necessary to work as part of a team or structured grouping.[35] It is significant that he saw his involvement with his fellow *poblacion* dwellers as his primary commitment; it was this, rather than the teaching work, which was to lead him to his final destiny.

Michael's involvement with *MAPU* may have been strengthened by his acquaintance with Nano Rojas. He had called on Nano with one of the sisters in Cerro Placeres in 1970. Nano, his wife, Juana, and their two children lived in a wooden shack with two other couples and an unmarried brother. To call it overcrowded was an understatement. Michael offered Nano and his family the prefab which the students would be vacating when eventually his house was completed. Nano and his family moved into it in mid-1971 and occupied it until 1975, dismantling and taking it with them to a new site in a land occupation in 1972.

Nano was a fruit and vegetable porter working for several firms which bought and sold fruit in Valparaiso market. The porters worked in the street with their shirts off on low pay. It was piece work and they had neither health insurance nor provision for a pension. With

Michael's encouragement Nano set up a vegetable and fruit porters' Union. From his experience in Las Habas Michael was familiar with the claims workers were entitled to make of their employers. He acted as secretary and took the minutes of the weekly meetings, held in a local restaurant. With his help they drew up a list of grievances demanding insurance, pension and holiday rights and the statutory bonuses for Christmas and Independence Day. They also demanded a pay increase from twenty cents to fifty cents per box carried. This was the sum Michael thought their work was worth and which the twenty-five firms employing them could afford to pay. Apart from an additional one of a share in the companies' profits, all the Union's claims were accepted. The new Government was, of course, on the side of Unions and legislated in their favour. It is hard to imagine that Michael's involvement endeared him to the owners.[36]

It became known in *CESCLA* that Michael had become a *MAPU* activist. Rodrigo Gonzalez considered him very radical but believed that he commanded respect for his transparent goodness and generosity rather than for the views he expressed.[37] The Director who succeeded Gonzalez in early 1973 had the impression that Michael was not really a political person at all, but that he thought he would be more useful as a member of a political party. He always wished to be of service: that was the basis of everything. *MAPU* offered a place where he would be with other Christians. Some elements in *MAPU* were more Marxist in tendency, others more Christian. The Christians sometimes felt that they were being used by the Marxists. Michael's answer was: 'No, we have to serve'. 'His was the kind face of *MAPU* with a tremendous love for his neighbour. Unlike many at the time he was never a political extremist'.[38] One of the *CESCLA* students, who got to know Michael and was a fellow member of *MAPU,* said of him: 'Michael had a very delicate and generous way of expressing himself with people: his attitude was one of trying to understand and to be of service. Everyone who knew him liked him very much'.[39]

During most of 1970 Michael had worked at Las Habas and lived with Patricio in Villa Berlin. For the first half of 1971, after Patricio's departure, he continued sharing the house with Willy Avaria. He still occasionally celebrated Mass with the Sisters, who mostly now went down to the parish church. Otherwise he celebrated it in the house with Willy, with whichever of the students was around and some invited neighbours. His Masses:

> always included dialogue which gave a strong feeling of solidarity, joy and love to those who took part. They had a real sense of following Christ. Michael saw his work at Las Habas and later in *CESCLA* and the weekend building work on the new house in Progreso as the daily sacrifice taken up in the Mass. Sharing food and communicating with his fellow workers in the shipyard, with the *CESCLA* staff and students and his fellow *poblacion* dwellers in Placeres was for him communion.[40]

Michael's was not the only house being built in Buenos Aires Street. There were others, on both sides of the new road. Mains water was brought to Poblacion Progreso about this time and each householder was expected to dig ten metres of trench for the piping or pay someone else to do it. Michael dug the trench in front of his own property and helped his neighbours with theirs. As it happened the trench was wrecked by the 1971 earthquake and had to be re-dug, this time with a mechanical digger. One of his near neighbours was building a house for himself and his family a few yards up the road. When he had finished it, he asked Michael to bless his new house. Michael was happy to do so, but without ceremony:

> He insisted that we must be what we feel. He asked us all

to sit down and then asked each of us what we were feeling, first me, then my wife, then our two eldest children who were there too. When we said how happy we felt to be in our own house as a family, he said we could give thanks to God for that. And that was the blessing.[41]

Michael's house was virtually complete at the time of the serious earthquake which occurred on the night of the 7th July 1971, in Valparaiso and did much damage to the city. The design and construction of the new house proved effective: it did not suffer any damage. Shortly after this he moved in together with Manuel and Jaime who transferred from the prefab. Lautaro had married in March 1971, and moved away. Willy Avaria stayed on alone in Patricio's old house for a few months until he also married, in November 1971. In a speech after the wedding which he celebrated, Michael, with characteristic humour, told the bride that her husband was a good cook but never washed up or put the rubbish out.[42] In spite of the religious earnestness there had evidently been some domestic arguments during their time together.

The house in Buenos Aires Street had all its occupants needed except an indoor bathroom. They had to make do with washing in the kitchen. A shower was planned but was not installed by the time of the Coup two years later. They had mains water and Michael and the students had dug a deep cess pit for drainage.

The three occupants of the new house became, for a few months at least, an informal community, so fulfilling the original aim of the students in coming to Placeres, though there was no fixed routine and each of them was free to organise his own life. They ate together sometimes and on these occasions reflected on the Bible. At night, when they were in the house, they would pray together before going to bed. The method was again to take a Bible passage, comment briefly on it, pray and then they said good-night. Michael was able to link whatever

Bible passage they were reflecting on to the practical realities of everyday life. As a consequence of their reflections they would sometimes decide on some action to undertake the next day. The students themselves would occasionally become caught up in abstract discussions, for example, about the notion of eternal life.[43] Such speculations were not of interest to Michael for whom they represented an evasion of Christian duty.

Indeed Michael was so single minded in his commitment to working for others that he sometimes expressed impatience with the more leisurely attitude of the students. Jaime used to spend half an hour a day doing Karate exercises in the house. Michael criticized him for wasting time and energy which could have been given to the poor who needed, for example, water and light. Jaime should presumably have been outside digging in water pipes or wiring up their houses.[44] Mass had been

A typical section of Cerro Placeres

Cerro Placeres: Interior of the house of Michael's
neighbour, Luis Rodríguez

celebrated from time to time, mainly on Sundays in the
prefab when the students lived there. It happened less
frequently in the house.

With the commissioning of the new house Michael had
now completed his own progression into a new world. He

was now himself a *poblador* living among the other *pobladores* of Poblacion Progreso. The neighbour whose house he had blessed, Luis Rodríguez, regarded him as virtually a member of his family. He had his own chair in the corner of their living room and arrived after work with the customary sausages and eggs. Michael considered his salary as a lecturer at the University in *CESCLA* as far in excess of what he needed for himself. He found ways of redistributing it among his neighbours by giving them 'loans' when they were in need and also, to avoid paternalism, he paid them to do small jobs for him.[45] Nano Rojas was asked to level a piece of ground, on another occasion to construct a wooden fence.[46]

When he joined *MAPU* Michael became a member of a local Action Group[47] on Cerro Placeres. One of the first major activities his group engaged in was occasioned by the earthquake which not only damaged Valparaiso itself but caused devastation elsewhere in the Fifth Region. Homeless families arrived on Cerro Placeres looking for a small plot of land on which to make a new home. There was an uncultivated area above Poblacion Progreso belonging to a Religious Congregation. The homeless people occupied it but were turned away by the police, only to come back and reoccupy it the following night. The *MAPU* group worked on behalf of the new settlers, helping them set up their campsite — the first stage in the birth of a new *poblacion* — running a first aid clinic and providing hot food, blankets and moral support. At night there were camp fires and singing.

One of the land occupations of that time was planned by the *MAPU* group in Michael's house (though he may not himself have been present owing to work): Rodrigo Gonzalez, Jaime Contreras and Luis Rodríguez took part. When the time came, Michael himself led the occupation. He and many of the others carried Chilean flags. 'We all set out together, with women and children, and occupied the land. As soon as we were in possession the police moved us off, but each time we went back until eventually we stayed. Michael was always in front'.[48]

When, eventually, the refugees from the earthquake were left in peace to set up their camps in the areas they had occupied, there was a long delay in getting the land officially parcelled out in such a way that they could begin to build more permanent homes. This was because of the problem of ownership which had to be settled before they could remain there legally. The authorities seemed to be dragging their feet. The new settlers therefore took the initiative once more themselves. Accompanied by Michael, a group of about a hundred of them, including families with young children, went to the railway station at the bottom of Cerro Placeres and boarded a train bound for Santiago. There was no question of buying tickets: it was a protest occupation of the train, undertaken to force the pace of bureaucracy. The train was stopped at Yungay, the last station before Santiago. The station staff thought they had an armed insurrection on their hands and telephoned the police who arrived with riot shields, weapons and tear gas. When they discovered their mistake, an assistant minister from the Housing Ministry in Santiago was sent to talk to the protesters. He gave an undertaking to arrange the surveying, parcelling, legal transfer and registration of the land. The previous owners never made an appearance. The protesters were transported back to Cerro Placeres by coach.

On Christmas Day 1971, Michael celebrated the dawn Mass in a derelict building on one of the camp sites. He was accompanied by a Protestant pastor.[49]

NOTES

1. Villa Berlin had been established under the inspiration of an English priest, Fr Cyril Elton, who had close ties with the German business community in Valparaiso and persuaded them to provide funds to build the new *poblacion* as a cooperative housing estate.

2. Of the Congregation of *Notre Dame de Namur*. Patricio had lived on the edge of the cooperative housing estate at first, but when, later, there was a land occupation (*toma de terrenos*) he took a plot of land for himself and built a house. He found this a point of contact with his new neighbours, many of whom were Communists. It was a welcome change' from the highly organised life on the cooperative housing estate. The house was in Calle Coquimbo, Cooperativa Hamburgo, Villa Berlin.

3. Patricio Guarda 1991.

4. His title as Priest-in-Charge (*Vicario Economo*) of Peña Blanca remained officially in force until his suspension from the priesthood in August 1972.

5. Victor Bernal 1992.

6. From the Young Christian Workers (*J O C*) in Valparaiso where they had both known him until 1964. Willy had joined the Christian Democrat Party and been sent to Chile to study agronomy. He returned to Valparaiso to work with the Party, attending the secret meetings within Christian Democracy which resulted, in May 1969, in the formation of *MAPU*, which he joined. (Willy Avaria 1995).

7. *Instituto Nacional de Capacitacion Profesional — INACAP*

8. Memoir by Matilde Silva 1990.

9. Manuel Rojas 1990.

10. Mariano Puga 1990.

11. The area has not changed. In 1992 a small number of front doors in the streets around the port had notices saying 'private house' implying that the rest were *'maisons publiques'*.

12. Luis Herrera 1992. He was a fellow worker.

13. Norma Bernal 1992. She and her husband were the friends who helped.

14. Luis Herrera 1992.

15. Feliciano Gonzalez 1996. He was another worker at Las Habas. Under the Military *Junta* Las Habas was taken over by the Chilean Navy.

16. Norma Bernal 1992.

17. Michael banked his money and earnings with Patricio and the record of income and expenditure from October 1969 to June 1970 survives. This shows that purchase of the plot of land was completed on 27th February 1970 with the payment of 2,455 *escudos*.

18. The Christian community (*comunidad cristiana*) is, within the Catholic Church in Chile, a grouping of faithful who meet to celebrate Mass, often in secular surroundings and in an informal manner. In the end a chapel is often built to serve this community. Such communities are loosely under the ecclesiastical jurisdiction of the nearest parish, but in practice are largely independent. They form the normal Catholic presence in the *poblaciones*.

19. In 1990 a similar basic housing unit was available in Santiago at the *Hogar de Cristo* for £500.

20. A University lecturer in their Department, Rodrigo Gonzalez, put them in touch with another Catalan priest working in Quillota. This priest, Antonio Llido, who was also to die violently after the 1973 coup, went round the secondary schools in Quillota gathering children from poor homes who wanted to participate in the camp. The camp took place at the village of Cerro Mayaca. The food was paid for by the municipality of Quillota.

21. Carlos Barhoilet. According to Juana Rojas the house was actually designed by a colleague of his.

22. Jaime Contreras 1991.

23. For this resume I am indebted to Brian Loveman, op.cit.

24. Willy Avaria 1995. The Catalan priest was Ignacio Pujadas.

25. *Centro de Estudios y Capacitacion laboral.*

26. Michael discussed with Willy Avaria whether to accept this post. Willy himself had a new job at this time: he became General Secretary of the Municipal Housing Department (*Corporacion Regional de Servicios Habitacionales* or *Corhabit*) in Valparaiso.

27. Conversation with Rodrigo Gonzalez 1990. By then he was Head of Education for the Vth Region. Later he became Mayor of Viña del Mar.

28. *Universidad popular de verano.*

29. His name was Javier Martínez.

30. Javier Martínez 1992.

31. *Movimiento de Accion Popular Unitario.*

32. *Movimiento de la Izquierda Revolucionaria.*

33. Pepa Arangua.

34. Myrta Crocco 1990.

35. Pepo Gutíerrez 1992.

36. Nano Rojas 1996.

37. Rodrigo Gonzalez 1990.

38. Fernando Alvarado 1992.

39. Maximo Valdivia 1990.

40. Willy Avaria 1995.

41. Luis Rodríguez 1990.

42. Willy Avaria 1995.

43. Jaime Contreras 1992.

44. ibid.

45. Luis Rodríguez 1990. The following year, 1972, Michael's salary amounted to 130,609.80 *escudos* according to a declaration to the Revenue Inspectors.

46. Nano Rojas 1996.

47. *Grupo de Accion Politica* or *GAP.*

48. Nano Rojas 1996.

49. Juana de Rojas 1996.

CHAPTER SIX

RAISING THE STAKES (1972-1973)

At the beginning of 1972 Michael went with two of the Sisters and several families from Placeres on a twelve-day, Government sponsored, summer camp for *poblacion* dwellers. The camp took place on the coast between Coquimbo and La Serena. Accommodation, in huts, and full board were provided at a subsidised rate which the families were expected to pay back over a ten month period. Each neighbourhood council president was entitled to fill a coach with ten or so families from his own *poblacion*. Fifteen or sixteen coaches set off in convoy around eleven o'clock in the evening and travelled through the night. Owing to the political passions in Chile at the time, they had to pass quietly through at least one area on the way down Cerro Placeres for fear of stones being thrown at the coaches by local residents who opposed the Allende Government.

Many families, indeed, who could have enjoyed the holiday, chose not to go because they perceived it to be a form of Government propaganda involving political indoctrination. This was partly true. There were talks and films which were no doubt related to the political situation and to the aims of the Allende Government, but attendance at them was not compulsory. Those who went were happy to join in the chores of washing up, cleaning and tidying. They did minor repairs to the huts, such as replacing broken window panes, and were proud, at the end of the week, to have left the place clean and in excellent order.[1] The food was considered good. Whist drives and domino championships took place in the evenings. On some days there were excursions.

One of the excursions involved a train journey from Coquimbo to Vicuna. At a certain point on the journey there was a long, steady incline which the train climbed very slowly. Michael, who was travelling in a carriage with families from Placeres whom he knew well, stood up and said: 'O.K. folks, I'm off. *Ciao!*' And he got off the train, ran in slow motion along the track, letting the train move away ahead of him as if he couldn't keep up, shouting '*Ciao, Ciao*' to everyone inside and roaring with laughter. When the train had left him completely behind he suddenly put on a spurt, caught up the last carriage, got on again and greeted everyone joyfully.[2]

Besides Christmas and the summer holidays which follow, the other season when Chileans traditionally celebrate is around the *Fiestas Patrias* in September: on the 18th and 19th of that month the anniversary of Chile's Declaration of Independence is commemorated with open-air parties, traditional food and the dancing of the *cueca*. Always ready to play the clown, Michael threw himself into this with gusto. His dancing instructor was Manuel. The *cueca* is a complicated dance and he made efforts to master its various steps. Though he knew these steps more or less, he lacked the subtlety and grace of the people. His conspicuous height drew attention to the clumsiness of his footwork and he was the object of merriment, a merriment he encouraged by performing the gestures of the dance or *picardias* in the exaggerated manner of a caricature Englishman.[3]

At the end of 1971, a split in *MAPU* resulted in Rodrigo Gonzalez being called to Santiago to work at Party headquarters on its ruling body. In the reshuffle which followed the Director's departure, Michael became General Secretary and second-in-command of *CESCLA*. He now gave secondary level classes two or three times a week on the current state of affairs in Chile, especially on the new laws and changing political situation under the Allende Government. He was also responsible for some of the administration of *CESCLA* This responsibility was uncongenial and he tended to delegate it to his secretary. As a result there were occasional tensions and arguments between them. According to her he was annoyed when 'things were not as they ought to be'.[4] Michael's refusal to be submerged in practical administration created difficulties for his subordinates but freed him to extend his personal contact with the working people for whose benefit *CESCLA* existed.

Building on the popular response to the annual summer university it organised in the industrial Quillota — Calera region, *CESCLA* planned to set up an out-station in the area where courses could be given all year round. Michael was put in charge of this project. It was hoped that a permanent centre would eventually offer workers the same opportunities to matriculate and gain degrees as at the Catholic University in Valparaiso. As a preliminary measure, however, potential students were to be approached to find out what they felt they most needed. From March 1972, therefore, Michael spent two days each week away from the University, travelling round the Calera region, on foot or motor bike. He consulted householders in the *poblaciones*, listened to workers and trade union officials in the factories, mines and industrial works of the area. About six hundred questionnaires were distributed. The needs which these established turned out to include basic literacy, Chilean history, mathematics, physics, chemistry, mechanical skills, economics and social sciences, the last two being requested by union leaders.

With the help of a *CESCLA* colleague[5] and of other visiting members of staff from the University, Michael set up a centre which, through a whole range of evening classes, offered the courses he had been asked for. The project was aimed at increasing the ability of workers to understand and become involved in the running of their industry. It was the policy of the Allende Government to encourage such participation. If factory workers were to have a say in management, they needed the skills which the *CESCLA* centre aimed to provide and they needed to have some understanding of the economic and political situation of the country as a whole. Under new government legislation, five out of eleven members of the management board of nationalised companies or of companies placed under a government administrator had to be workers from the shop floor. Taking responsibility of this kind was not easy nor was it widely popular with the workers themselves. In addition to the management boards, there were other committees such as those concerned with welfare or health and safety which required informed and confident worker participation.

The *CESCLA* out-station was based in the industrial training school attached to a large cement factory. It had good facilities, including a swimming pool, which may have been an attraction. Melon Cement, the company which owned the factory and training school, exemplified the needs which the centre aimed to meet, for a little earlier on, after a dispute between the work force and employers, the Government had put the company under the control of an Administrator[6] part of whose agenda was to introduce workers to the board of management. The Administrator himself was a member of *MAPU* and was the Party's local candidate in the 1972 Congressional elections. The *CESCLA* centre was a project which reflected the guiding principles of *MAPU*. In setting it up, Michael also had the assistance of his friend and fellow party-member Lautaro Prado. Lautaro had spent the first year after his marriage as a Philosophy teacher and in 1972 joined the staff of *CESCLA*.

In June and July 1972, while Michael was making his preparations for setting up the centre, there was serious flooding and later an earthquake in the Calera region which left many families homeless. He travelled round on his bike taking medical supplies where they were most needed in the sub-zero temperatures of the winter. Many of the homeless had to find new land on which to set up house and there were some land occupations. With his experience from Cerro Placeres, Michael was an old hand at this and was able to offer encouragement and some practical support. An observer who saw the energy and generosity with which he worked in this crisis noticed also that the people he helped came to regard him as one of their own.[7]

At this period, also, in mid-1972, Myrta Crocco, the social work lecturer who had become a friend of Michael's, was doing field work in the region with twenty-five of her students from the Catholic University. The students were visiting a number of local industries including a fruit and vegetable canning plant, a seaweed-drying works, a timber mill and the Melon Cement factory. They spent time with the workers, joining them in study groups, and provided a readymade resource for Michael to draw on in setting up the *CESCLA* out-station.

Courses at the new Centre were open to all industrial workers in the region. Applications for admission opened in the *Teatro del Pueblo* in Calera. Four hundred workers signed on, far more than Michael had envisaged, more than had applied for the first *CESCLA* courses in Valparaiso. The workers, both men and women, were enthusiastic to learn. They begged Michael to become the centre's Director. He refused, fearing that his time and energies would be taken up in administration. They persisted and eventually persuaded him by assuring him that he could leave the administration to others and concentrate himself on the human side of things. His lecturer friend noted that he was not only respected, but loved and trusted by the local community, both industrial workers and *poblacion* dwellers. She and her students were considered to be outsiders, but Michael was definitely one of the community. There were the usual jokes about him, his physical appearance and manner, always affectionate.[8]

Myrta Crocco recalls the impression Michael made on her own students when they worked with him. They were middle-class girls who had chosen to do social work studies in the first place because they wanted to become home visitors but, because of the university reforms, they were ending up, sometimes reluctantly, as social workers. So they were not always entirely committed to what they were doing. Both she and Michael, however, persuaded them to see the point of working with the poorest levels of society. Melon Cement provided accommodation for the girls and for the organisers of the *CESCLA* centre to live in. One night the girls, who slept in a dormitory, overheard Michael, Myrta and a colleague discussing how they might persuade them to work with greater commitment. They were affected by what Michael said and got the message. Michael also changed their attitude to the Church. They mostly believed that the Church was out of touch and not committed to social justice. But Michael, a priest, was clearly a human being like them, with similar concerns, equally exhausted by the work, equally critical of what he saw. He was extremely direct in relating to others, sometimes to the point of seeming rude,[9] but there was absolutely no doubt regarding his dedication, not that he spoke about it, but he lived it and the girls were in awe of him. They would ask: 'What would Michael have done in these circumstances?' And when they overslept and were late getting to work they were anxious that he should not know about it. He was not particularly close and familiar and they might have been put off by him: his example, however, exerted a powerful influence over them.[10]

The 'awe' felt by the girls probably reflected

Myrta's own feelings as a final incident she recounts reveals. At a general meeting of all the workforce of Melon Cement at which she and Michael were both present, a sixty-year-old man stood up and said: 'I have worked here for forty years. This is the first time I have spoken. I wish to speak of my work: I see how important it is'. As the old man spoke Myrta noticed that Michael's eyes filled with tears.[11]

Michael's work for *CESCLA*, and, in particular, his efforts at Calera which went far beyond the strict requirements of contract, were motivated by a commitment to the project, seemingly made realisable by the election of Allende, of giving power and dignity to that half or majority of the population whom he saw as exploited members of the human family. In his case it was the conscious commitment of a follower of Christ, but for him any selfless struggle on the part of professedly non-Christian Marxists made them more Christ-like than so-called Christians who were greedy and defensive of their privileges. This was the reason why he had become a *MAPU* militant.

Most members of the *CESCLA* staff in the University, from the Director down, belonged to a political action group run on MAPU principles. While much of Michael's day-to-day work was a matter of individual initiative, he shared with his colleagues a corporate sense of purpose in carrying forward whatever practical projects he was engaged on. In his home base in Poblacion Progreso the local Political Action Group was more tightly knit. Here Michael was part of a team which met and planned its activities several times a week.

Leadership of the meetings was shared between Lautaro, Manuel and Michael. The business in hand was usually of a practical character, but some of the meetings were devoted to political education. The group included several new recruits from the *poblacion* and these were introduced to the language and theory of Marxism. Explanations were given of terms such as 'added value', the value added to the capital invested in a product by the labour involved in its production, which led on to the question of how this added value was distributed. Terms such as this were taught in the political education sessions so that blue-collar workers might come to value themselves and be accorded greater dignity by others. The political education sessions also contained frequent and ongoing political analysis of the situation in Chile with resultant discussion. One of the novice members, not yet a fully fledged *MAPU* militant, (this rank had to be earned), voiced the need of some military training so that they could defend themselves in the event of a military crackdown - always known to be a possibility. He had just finished his military service with the Chilean Marines and was perhaps more realistic about the way things would turn out than the other members. In spite of *MAPU*'s official endorsement of the armed struggle in extreme circumstances, the other members of the group told him not to be crazy.[12]

The Progreso Action Group made a practical contribution to the life and amenities of the *poblacion*. In July 1971 it had been closely involved in the occupation of land by families made homeless by the earthquake. In 1972-3 its members undertook more humdrum tasks such as preparing stretches of road for surfacing and building concrete stairways down gullies so that people could reach their homes without sliding in the winter mud. In the neighbourhood Council, especially, they galvanised members to petition the municipal authorities for new amenities such as street lighting. On behalf of the Council they set up a volunteer fire brigade. It had a 'station', but equipment was primitive. Fires were usually the result of kitchen stoves bursting into flame or of over-exuberant barbecues. The alarm was raised by word of mouth, the brigade called by shouting along the road. They put the fires out with buckets of water and by beating them with blankets and branches.[13] A youth centre was also set up by the group, in a private house. It catered for fifteen- to twenty-year-olds and may have been thought of as a source of recruitment. Fiestas and football matches were its principal occupations. Perhaps the most significant and high profile activity taken on by the Action Group, however, was its involvement in the local Provision and Price Committee.[14]

Since well before the time of Allende every *poblacion* had a neighbourhood Council of which all adult householders, men and women, were members. They paid a subscription and elected a president, treasurer, secretary, auditors and delegates to accompany officers when these made contact with the municipal authorities or presented petitions to them. Michael was elected as an auditor for the Progreso Council. The handling of money can be a particularly delicate matter among needy people and they trusted him to provide impartial and accurate oversight of the accounts. The neighbourhood Councils also elected, when food shortages became a problem in 1972, a committee to oversee the supply of basic foods at fair prices to the area. These were the Provision and Price Committees. Each neighbourhood had one. Michael was elected as President of the Committee for Poblacion Progreso. From his experience with the owner of the foodstore in Peña Blanca and perhaps going back earlier still, he had always felt strongly about tradesmen making what he saw as undue profits on household essentials at the expense of *poblacion* dwellers. As a *MAPU* militant he may also have been keen to support the Provision and Price Committee which *MAPU* considered to be its invention. Over and above his own enthusiasm for the new Committee, Michael's election as its President by the other members of the neighbourhood Council suggests that he was recognised as honest and fair by the majority of his neighbours who were by no means all in agreement with his political views.

Provision and Price Committees were brought in by the Allende Government as a weapon with which to combat the hoarding and black market sale of food by shopkeepers. Though the first year of Allende's Government had been economically successful, a shortage of agricultural produce in Chile necessitated expensive imports which in turn led to balance of payments problems and inflation. Basic food items were kept artificially cheap by price controls. But there was a threat of shortages. Lorry owners, on whom the country depended for food distribution, were concerned lest their small, private businesses be taken over by the State. So they went on strike in August and September 1972 and again in July and August 1973. As distribution became more difficult, there was a good excuse for shopkeepers to claim shortages. Sometimes this was genuine, but often it was a pretext to sell for high prices to the well-off who, provided they could pay, were allowed to buy as much as they pleased. The poor found the shops empty of food for sale at the lower, official, price.

The Committee was intended to provide a locally based system of rationing and fair distribution of those basic foodstuffs included in what was known as 'the people's shopping basket'. Among these commodities were sugar, rice, cooking oil, tea, instant coffee, condensed milk, flour, meat, dried milk powder, some items of fresh fruit and vegetables. A member of the Committee regularly checked the price of these items at all the retail shops in its area. Purchases by the shopkeepers from wholesalers were undertaken with a Committee member present. In this way it was known what quantity of oil, rice, sugar or flour and the rest the retailer was buying. It could then be checked that what appeared for

114

sale in his shop corresponded to the amount he had bought at the wholesaler. In January 1973, the *MAPU* Minister for the Economy introduced a Government monopoly in the distribution and marketing of thirty commodities through the already existing Provision and Price Committees. From then on the basic food items could only be obtained legally from State depots.

In practice things did not work out as they were supposed to. Committee number 93 of Valparaiso, the Poblacion Progreso one, catered for five hundred and seventy people. The member responsible for supervising the collection of meat belonged to the right wing National Party. Under his supervision no meat was being made available for ordinary householders. When he was questioned at a meeting, he claimed that the State depot had none left when he got there. He was possibly selling it on the black market though this could not be proved, but at least he was shown to be negligent, on his own admission, by not getting to the depot early enough. So the task was handed over to Michael.

The meat had to be collected once a week. Being better organised or more disciplined than the National Party member, Michael arrived at the depot in Valparaiso by 5 a.m., and always brought back enough meat for the five hundred and seventy mouths he was responsible for in Poblacion Progreso. The meat was imported, boned, from the People's Republic of China. The ration for each person was a quarter of a kilo per week. The van belonged to a butcher, who did not himself go to the depot. Michael and one helper loaded it up and afterwards washed down the van. It was a dirty, greasy job. When they arrived back a queue of women was waiting for them, even though queuing was not necessary: there was enough for everyone. Before being distributed the meat was cut up by the butcher who had paid for it. Each housewife produced her ration ticket and paid a fair price.   The butcher made a profit and had most of his work done for him.

If the Provision and Price Committee succeeded with meat distribution in Progreso, with other food basics things were not so efficient or fair. The problem was that the Committees were elected by the neighbourhood Councils and members of political parties opposed to the Government could equally well be elected as *MAPU* or Socialists or Communists.   Christian Democrats and the National Party had no interest in making the Committees work.[15] In fact some of those elected were the very tradesmen whom the Committee was supposed to be supervising.   Under the guise of the Committee they continued to claim shortages at the wholesaler and sell on the black market in their shop.   There were frequent denunciations and rows about this.   On one occasion Michael publicly read out at a meeting the dates, names of the owners and registration numbers of the vehicles, and the quantities of groceries each had collected from the wholesaler and which had apparently not been or only partially been delivered.   Those present threatened him with violence until the *MAPU* militants went in and stood by him. He was able to produce these with the assistance of friends at the market and elsewhere who checked exactly what was being despatched.   The shopkeepers were furious.

Continual battle raged between those who took the Committee seriously and the rest, especially the political Right, who wanted to wreck it.   A Progreso shopkeeper was denounced in the neighbourhood Council because people were coming in smart cars to her house from Viña and paying six times the official price for cooking oil. The shopkeeper was forced to accept a Committee inspector to check her incomings and outgoings.   Those who owned their own businesses, who were mostly of the Right, resented interference of this kind.   The Left believed that some of the tradesmen were only interested in using the shortages to make themselves rich. Feelings rose so high that threats of murder were not uncommon.[16]

The various Provision and Price Committees on Cerro Placeres were each responsible for supplying their own *poblacion.* At general meetings and, sometimes, at the wholesalers or State depot in Valparaiso, tensions arose between the Committees themselves. The one person who managed to keep calm in these situations was Michael: eventually he was elected Chairman of all the Committees in Placeres, a further sign of the extent to which he was trusted. It was a poisoned chalice, however: partly because it was impossible to coordinate what was an inherently disunited organization trying to bring order into an increasingly difficult and tense situation; partly, also, because it raised his profile in Placeres and he was to become a marked man on whom one or two of the tradesmen would happily take revenge. It is not surprising that some of them spoke of him as the Red Priest, and that in the interrogation of another *MAPU* activist after the Coup, a Naval Intelligence officer referred to him as the priest who stirred up the rabble.[17]

Certain people, usually political opponents connected with local tradesmen, professed to be scandalised by a priest having a party political affiliation. Such a person was neither fish nor fowl.[18] Some shouted abuse at Michael as a foreigner when he walked by. In the face of this Michael always remained calm. Those on the side of the Government, on the other hand, were impressed by the fact that Michael, as a priest, was so down-to-earth and practical, that he was in touch with the concerns of the people and not aloof in some religious world. They were also impressed by his 'priestly' behaviour: by the fact that when he was insulted he did not react with anger himself. At meetings when an opponent became heated and abusive and Michael remained calm, his fellow *MAPU* members told him he should show anger himself. His reply was always: 'No, leave him alone. He doesn't yet understand'.[19]

The same self control was evident at a public meeting which Michael attended at the Velarde Theatre in Valparaiso in June 1973. General Bachelet, an Army officer whom Allende had brought into the Government as Finance Minister as part of an attempt at compromise with the Opposition, was speaking about the 'people's shopping basket', not exactly the one with which the Provision and Price Committees were concerned,. but a list of items used to gauge the cost of living. There was strong feeling on this issue. Bachelet insisted on including cars and fridges on the list of popular goods. Michael put it to him from the floor that cars and fridges were hardly popular. The people's shopping basket should include only those everyday items which were expected to be within the range of a worker's weekly wage packet. He spoke with restraint and courtesy but, owing to the tension which his remarks exacerbated, he was expelled from the hall.[20] It was an act of courage since his views were now unacceptable to the Allende Government itself: it had dropped *MAPU,* sacrificing it to the need to compromise and slow down the pace of reform. Michael was, in any case, incapable of understanding political compromise. For him, if a thing was right, it should be pursued regardless of opposition.

In 1972 and 1973, with the *CESCLA* work in Valparaiso and Calera and growing responsibilities with the Provision and Price Committee, the pace of Michael's life accelerated increasingly. He still found time, however, to visit the Bernal family on Monday evenings when he got back from the University. The routine remained the same: the time of silence and the reflection on Scripture were more important now than ever.

We wanted that moment to dialogue with God, with

Him and with each other, because everyone was terribly wrought up and tense. There was no time for anything. It was all politics, politics, politics. People were on edge, frightened and ill. There were many nasty rumours circulating. On one occasion Michael told us that we shouldn't read so many articles written by Church people which only put across the point of view of the rich. We were to pray constantly and live as our Church of the Gospel, in the present moment and circumstances we found ourselves in. We didn't need a Church which handed us everything ready-made, telling us what to do, but we were to live the Gospel out in our own lives, not let our life pass us by without being aware of it. If we were hungry — and we often were because of the food shortages — we were to feel the hunger. And when people came to the door who had nothing to eat, and if I had some food, I had to share it with them. Michael himself shared a great deal. He used to say: 'I was keeping such and such to eat but when I got home there was nothing there: they had come in and eaten everything'. 'They' were neighbours who hadn't got anything. So he came and ate with us if there was any food here'.[21]

In spite of the work of the Provision Committees there were serious food shortages. Michael offered advice to his friends in these circumstances: 'He used to say that the Christian should be creative and resourceful when things were hard. I paid attention to this on one occasion when there was no bread and no flour. An idea occurred to me and I went off and bought three kilos of wheat. With the grinder I had in the kitchen I was able to extract flour and make some bread as well as give the husks to our rabbits'.[22]

After their departure for the south in December 1970, Michael kept loosely in touch with Patricio and Marie-Claire. His first letter to them, written on 12th February 1971, is a brief note about dates for a possible visit by him to Concepcion. Another letter, dated 10th August 1972, gives an idea of his work and political concerns of the moment, concerns which now seem esoteric and excessively ideological:

> I hope you are both well, in your work and in general. I have quite a lot of work with the *CESCLA* centre in Calera, classes in Valparaiso and courses in trade unionism, provision and price committee formation etc. The political situation is confused. Here we fed up to the back teeth with the Political Commission of *MAPU* in Santiago for having ordered a withdrawal from the People's Assembly of Concepcion. It appears that Gazmuri and Correa in Santiago are not very honest and have been influenced too much by the Communists and other Government Parties in Santiago. I agree that 'People's Assembly' is too Socialist a term for this stage in the process; it could have been called Workers', Peasants' and Students' Council. What was being attempted was to give a voice to the people, denouncing but not supplanting the bourgeois Parliament.
>
> Your prefab in Progreso has passed into the hands of Nano and Juana Rojas and their children. They were already occupying it and they moved it to a camp site in upper Placeres. This happened by order of a Housing Department official. They didn't have another prefab and were living in one whose owner didn't need it, so it has disappeared. Fair enough I believe. They will pay for it. They are not at all well off. A pity that it will never be the same as when we put it up. Regards and see you in the summer when, God willing, I may go south. Miguel.

On 10th June 1972, Manuel Rojas' marriage took place in Michael's house. There had been a civil ceremony a month before. Now the couple, Manuel and his bride, Delfina, each made promises in their own words. Michael celebrated Mass and communion was given under both kinds. The party went on all night with dancing to guitar and accordion. From his salary Michael paid a builder to construct them a permanent house and he also provided them with a monthly allowance. Theirs was the household he visited more than any other. He arrived after work, as always with tinned sausages, eggs and occasionally bananas. The children were delighted when he arrived and would get up and go to the table to eat. The house had its bedroom area partitioned off by curtains. Neighbours' children who came would get a fright when Michael loomed up like a monster over the top of the partition. Sometimes they all went for a walk to a nearby ravine which was covered in lush vegetation. These were moments of relaxation from work and anxiety.[23]

The jokes with children in the Rojas' house were characteristic of Michael. He had the ability to converse with old and young alike. Children readily approached him. He always found something funny to say and they were invariably delighted. As usual he played on the strangeness of his physique. 'What's the air like up there?' a child in the street asked him as he walked by. 'Very good', he replied. 'What's it like down there among the ants?' The child could count on a good natured response.[24]

The jokes and clowning gave Michael a rapport with the very young, he was close to the Action Group members and their families, especially the young recruits, he had his regular ports of call in the *poblacion* such as the Bernal or Rodríguez households and there were his professional colleagues and auxiliary staff in *CESCLA*. But it is unlikely that any of these friendships could be described as intimate or even as fully equal relationships. Once Patricio and Marie-Claire left, Michael was in this sense on his own. Even those who lived or had lived with him, Manuel, Jaime and Lautaro, were much younger and to some extent in awe of him. However much he rejected his own social background there remained wide differences of culture and education between him and those among whom he had chosen to live. This was not something Michael would have regretted or even perhaps acknowledged. He had chosen to leave his own class and culture behind. He would always, in any case, have been personally reserved in his relations with others. But in this environment it was even more difficult for any kind of deep personal friendship to arise.

With Lautaro and Manuel married and living with their new families, Michael had only Jaime as company in the new house in Buenos Aires Street. In 1972 Jaime was working at the University and returning home in the evening, but in 1973, he was involved in MAPU activities in Viña and returned only occasionally to sleep. During the whole of this period Michael was himself away a great deal in Calera. When he returned home it was usually to an empty house. His friends in Placeres continued to look on him as a priest and so for them his solitude was not so remarkable. But there was no human support from the Church, although he still saw one or two priest acquaintances from time to time. In the world of the *pobladores* in general a solitary priest was an anomaly. The ultimate step in Michael's journey into his new world was not accomplished when he moved into his own house in Buenos Aires Street. It would be taken only when he changed from living on the edge of other people's marriages and families to having one of his own.

Sometime after mid-1971 Michael decided that it was right for him to think of marriage as a possibility. The example of Patricio and Marie-Claire was a positive one. He did not think that all priests should marry but in his own case the vocation to marriage arose from the context in which he lived. He believed that marriage was his vocation now, before there was anyone in the offing who might be his wife.[25] One day in 1972 he met a priest who had been with him at seminary in a restaurant in Viña. Michael told him that he wanted to marry. There was nobody in particular he had in mind but he made out a list of the characteristics that the woman he was looking for would possess. She would have to be a spiritual person and committed to work for social justice. 'There was nothing about feelings', his friend commented, 'it was all very abstract and logical'.[26]

As a teacher in the University Michael encountered female students in a way he had not experienced before. He started inviting them out to tea and the cinema. Then there was a member of staff in the social work department whom he saw regularly for a time. He described her to Norma Bernal as sensible, serious and down-to-earth. He was seriously courting her. Manuel and Delfina Rojas gave him some instruction on how to conduct the courtship.[27] But, according to Norma Bernal, he was not in love with the girl.[28]

According to one of the Dominican Sisters, Michael was still celebrating Mass from time to time in the chapel next to their house and people were confused when they saw him out with a girl.[29] Whether word of this reached the bishop is not known but on the 8th August 1972, Don Emilio Tagle signed a decree of suspension from the priesthood in the following terms:

> Michael Woodward Y. having manifested the intention of abandoning the exercise of his priestly ministry, as from to-day I decree the suspension of all faculties for the exercise of his priesthood and, since he has not petitioned to be reduced to the lay state, he remains under the obligation to fulfil the norms laid down by the Church for clerics, in particular those of praying the Divine Office and of celibacy.

It was sent with an accompanying letter by the Chancellor of the Diocese,[30] addressed to Señor Miguel Woodward Y.

It is not clear why Bishop Tagle chose this particular moment to suspend Michael. It is indeed possible that he had heard rumours of a girl friend. But Tagle was kind to his priests, even those he considered were going astray, and was not a man to take abrupt action for what he would have seen as a human lapse. But Marxism in general and the Allende Government in particular were his *bêtes noires*. Michael's involvement with the Provision and Price Committee was far more likely to have provoked his anger.[31] It remains possible that rumours of a liaison were a pretext, but it seems unlikely. The bishop's reference to Michael's 'decision to abandon his priestly ministry', according to one Church authority,[32] relates to his departure in late 1969 from the parish of Peña Blanca. The official reason for his suspension by the bishop seems to be that he had chosen without authorization to live outside canonical structures. The particular timing may have been due to nothing more significant than the slow moving of ecclesiastical bureaucracy, but most probably it was caused by the bishop's disapproval of his political involvement.

It is likely that once Bishop Tagle became aware of diocesan priests being active in political parties supporting the Government, he would not tolerate their situation. In the following year he took action against Michael's friend, Antonio Llido, who was a member of the extreme left wing *MIR*. As a priest he worked in a *poblacion* in Quillota. His chapel was officially under the authority of the local parish priest.[33] He and Tagle jointly asked him to resign because of his involvement with *MIR*. The people in his section of the parish protested and his priest friends from the Industrial Mission Team, including Michael, travelled to Quillota one Sunday to show solidarity with Llido. They took part in a protest march from the chapel in the *poblacion* to the parish church. Two hundred people arrived at the church where an evening Mass was in progress. The marchers entered in time for one of them to add to the bidding prayers one for justice for Antonio Llido. A young seminarian who was present, thinking it was an occupation (which was not the intention of the protestors), telephoned the police. The demonstrators were persuaded to leave the church and assembled in the square outside where they were joined by more people from the town. One of the Group[34] addressed the crowd from a bandstand in the centre of the square. The following day the Diocesan Priests' Council met in Valparaiso and issued a statement to the press censuring and threatening with canonical penalties the priests who had taken part in the protest.[35]

Michael's reaction to his own suspension is not recorded. Jaime Contreras, who was living with him, was not aware of it, nor was his friend Pepo Gutiérrez. In all probability he did not mention it except on one occasion when it was necessary. Later in 1972 a *CESCLA* colleague asked him to perform the marriage ceremony for himself and his wife. Michael replied: 'I would like to do the wedding but unfortunately I have been suspended by the diocese'. He explained further: 'I would happily marry you because once a priest, always a priest. When we enter the service of God it continues till death'. But in the event he did not do so since the marriage would have been invalid in civil law.[36]

According to Manuel Rojas, Michael continued to celebrate Mass from time to time both in Manuel's house and in his own, right up till the time of the coup. Nor did he ever express antipathy or rancour towards Don Emilio. For him the people he lived and worked among were all important. Ecclesiastical structures were by now entirely remote.[37]

Sometime in mid-1972 Michael met a secondary school teacher and church catechist whom we shall call Isabel though that was not her name. An understanding and mutual appreciation grew between them which left room for the spiritual as well as the emotional and physical. They spent Sundays together, going on picnics, which was what Michael most liked. Love letters were exchanged. They discussed marriage, in particular how they could remain faithful to each other in freedom, without becoming slaves to the other's egotism. Later Isabel visited him from time to time in his office at the University. His secretary noted that she was clearly in love with him. She supposed he was also in love with her, though he did not show it. It was not in his character to show his feelings but she felt that he must be serious.[38]

On one occasion Michael brought Isabel to the Bernals' house in Placeres. Victor Bernal had been upset when he heard that Michael intended to marry. He asked him why he wished to do this since he was a priest. Michael replied: 'I am forty years old'. Victor asked again why he was giving up the priesthood; it was a big blow for the Bernals. He said he could not bear being alone any longer. He had seen other priests with the same conflict. He had been glad when Patricio married Marie-Claire. He felt cut off in his heart. And he said it was the fault of the faithful that priests felt so lonely. When Michael brought Isabel to their house, however, they thought she 'seemed a child but it was as if they were destined for one another. She suited him because she was able to understand him: he was very different from us'.[39] It seems unlikely that Michael blamed the faithful for the loneliness of priests. Neither the language nor the sentiment are characteristic. More probably the Bernals themselves felt some kind of guilt.

In January 1973, Michael and Isabel announced their engagement in a circular letter to the family in Europe. In their minds the engagement was to be a serious preparation for marriage, not an anticipation of it. Michael had once told Norma Bernal: 'I shall never sleep with a woman who is not my wife. And for her to become my wife I must love her. Love comes first of all'.[40]

In late July 1973, as tension was building up in the country as a whole, the Catholic University of Valparaiso was seized and occupied by students of the Right. Political opponents saw (and see) this occupation as instigated by naval officers as a preparatory measure anticipating the coup which was already being planned. The University buildings are in a strategic position on the road out of Valparaiso towards Viña. Whatever the truth of that allegation, the University was briefly reoccupied by the Left before being taken once again by the Right who remained in possession until the coup. The Director of *CESCLA*[41] arranged to have some discussions with the Christian Democrat Rector of the University in an attempt to restore the situation to normal. This approach offended other *MAPU* members who fell out among themselves. Michael took no part in these arguments because 'that was not how things ought to be'. From now on, however, he withdrew increasingly from *CESCLA* to concentrate on work in the *poblacion*.[42]

During the winter months of 1973 the atmosphere in and around Valparaiso became ever more explosive. Some naval personnel, stationed in the port, who had contacts with the Socialist Party, were accused of mutiny and imprisoned. There were noisy demonstrations on their behalf by students and workers of the Left, in particular a march in Valparaiso on 4th September, the anniversary of Allende's election. One witness,[43] travelling from Valparaiso to Viña that day, had to make the journey in three separate vehicles owing to roadblocks. He returned on a train packed with left wing passengers celebrating the anniversary. The train had been commandeered and 'occupied'. As it reached the point on its route near the University of Santa Maria, there was a pitched battle with stones between its occupants, many of whom were on the roof, and local supporters of the political Right.

At this time, too, paramilitaries began to emerge on to the streets of Valparaiso. Their appearance was heralded by the sound of boots running in step. They wore balaclavas and masks, carried sticks, and advanced intimidatingly, eight abreast, in groups of several hundred. Confrontations with the police were frequent but did not stop them.[44] Valparaiso and the whole country waited anxiously.

NOTES

1. Norma Bernal 1992.
2. Victor and Norma Bernal 1992.
3. Willy Avaria 1995.
4. Georgina Arangua 1996.
5. Juan Aldana
6. Vicente Sota
7. Myrta Crocco 1992
8. Myrta Crocco 1992. His *CESCLA* colleague, Juan Aldana, was also impressed by the 'strength of character and conviction with which Michael carried out his work. Organization based on good social relations was what mattered most. He was positively aggressive in opposing any tendency to bureaucracy: there was a lot of   that around, both on the Left and on the Right in Chile at the time. Above all he was always in touch with the working people themselves'.
9. As on the occasion when Myrta Crocco introduced a Brazilian couple to him: 'What are you doing here?', he asked, 'in my opinion you should have stayed in Brazil'. They were refugees. (Myrta Crocco 1992).
10. Myrta Crocco 1990.
11. ibid.
12. Eduardo Catalan 1992.
13. After the Coup the 'station' was moved down the hill to Villa Berlin and presented with a fire engine from Germany.
14. *Junta de Abastecimiento y Precios (JAP)*
15. The Christian Democrat Party, which had supported Allende's endorsement as President in 1970, had by now become critical of the Government and joined the Opposition.
16. Eduardo Catalan 1992.
17. *el cura que revolvia el gallinero.*

18. *ni chicha ni limonada.*
19. Eduardo Catalan 1992.
20. ibid.
21. Norma Bernal 1992.
22. ibid.
23. Delfina Rojas 1992.
24. Eduardo Catalan 1990.
25. This was the view of Willy Avaria. (1995).
26. Gonzalo Aguirre 1992.
27. Manuel Rojas 1990.
28. Norma Bernal 1992.
29. Soeur Bernardette Vincart 1991.
30. Fr Jaime Astorga (from the Diocesan Archives).
31. Carlos Camus 1992.
32. Enrique Barilari 1992.
33. Rene Pianori.
34. Pepo Gutiérrez.
35. Pepo Gutiérrez 1992.
36. '*Yo me siento plenamente capacitado para casarte y lo haria con mucho gusto*'. (Maximo Valdivia 1990).
37. Jaime Contreras 1991.
38. Georgina Arangua 1996.
39. Norma Bernal 1992.
40. ibid.
41. Fernando Alvarado, a *MAPU* activist.
42. Georgina Arangua 1996.
43. Pepo Gutiérrez 1992.
44. Carlos Ramirez Rojas 1996.

CHAPTER SEVEN

SHOWDOWN (11th September 1973)

Each year in early September a task force of the United States Navy carried out manoeuvres with the Chilean fleet. There was nothing special about this: it sailed round the Continent doing the same with the navies of other friendly countries whose shores it passed. On the afternoon of Monday, 10th September, 1973, the Defence Minister and supporters of the Allende Government were relieved to hear that the Chilean fleet had left the port of Valparaiso to meet up with the Americans further north. What they did not know was that this was a subterfuge providing a cloak of normality to last-minute preparations for the Coup. The fleet in fact sailed west, not north, waited below the horizon until nightfall and then, under cover of darkness, returned to port. Admiral of the Fleet Raúl Montero, the only Commander-in-Chief in the Armed Forces who remained loyal to the President, was taken prisoner in Valparaiso sometime on the Monday and held incommunicado. His position was taken over by Admiral Merino, who had agreed to the Coup.

Reveille in the Marines' barracks in Valparaiso sounded at 5am on Tuesday,11th September. At 5.45 Admiral Merino ordered 'Operation Silence': telephone exchanges and radio transmitters were seized and communication with the rest of the country cut off. At 6am Marines (Naval land forces) occupied railway and bus stations and secured water, gas and electricity supplies. By 6.45am the Navy had control of all key communications points in the City and Province. During the rest of the day they moved out into factories, working class areas, the Universities and Government offices.

From this catastrophic moment until his death ten or eleven days later it is possible to establish the general sequence of Michael Woodward's movements. Encounters are remembered by several witnesses. His friend Javier Martínez[1] lived with his parents half way up Cerro Placeres. Javier's father, a railway worker, left home for work early on the Tuesday morning. On his way down to the bottom of Cerro Placeres, where the railway from Valparaiso to Viña passes along the shore, he came up against a road block manned by Marines and was forced to return home. Javier then went out into the street, taking the opposite direction up towards the top of the Cerro. As he approached Poblacion Progreso he met Michael. Soon they were joined by a crowd of local residents all trying, from what snippets of information they had, to piece together some picture of what was going on.

Between 8.30 and 9am Michael walked up to Manuel and Delfina Rojas' house, tapped on the window and was let in. He told them the Marines had set up a roadblock and it was impossible to get to Valparaiso. That was the last they saw of him for several days.[2] At mid-morning he visited the house of some members of his Action Group.[3] Where he went next is not known.

At 8am President Allende in Santiago broadcast to the Chilean people, telling them that part of the Navy had revolted in Valparaiso, but that Santiago was quiet. Very soon afterwards, discovering that Army, Air Force and Police officers had joined the rebellion with their units, he broadcast again saying that he would never resign as President, ordering the workers to mobilize, gather in their factories and stand by their Government.

At about 8.30 came a proclamation of military rule from the *Junta*. Citing the grave social and moral crisis, the rise in paramilitary groups, the inability of the Government to prevent chaos and the inevitability of civil war, it demanded the President's resignation and expressed its own determination to free the country from the

131

'Marxist yoke' and restore 'institutionality'. It was signed by Pinochet for the Army, Merino for the Navy, Leigh for the Air Force and Mendoza for the Police.

At 9am the Moneda Palace, official residence of the President, was surrounded by Army tanks. At 9.30 Allende broadcast his last declaration to the Chilean people telling them they should defend themselves but not sacrifice their lives. He spoke of the treason of the Armed Forces and declared his faith that 'sooner rather than later the great avenues will open once again along which free citizens will march in order to build a better society'.

At 9.30 the Army's guns opened up on the Palace and, under this cover, infantry units advanced. All but the President's personal Guard and close companions left. It was not until about ten minutes to twelve that the aerial attack began. British-built Hawker Hunter planes dived over the Palace releasing rockets with perfect aim. The building was an inferno. Army units stormed in. Allende was found lying dead on the grand staircase beneath the statue of Chile's first President, Bernardo O'Higgins, most probably shot by his own hand with the Soviet machine gun presented to him by Fidel Castro. By twenty past two in the afternoon it was all over.

Whether it was a wise decision or not, at this stage Michael chose to stay away from his house and go into hiding. He had made enemies of some of the local tradesmen: they would have been relieved and delighted by the Coup and might well denounce him to the new authorities as a political activist of the former regime. They may have wanted to settle scores with the man who had denounced them as profiteers. Until 11th September the law had been on his side: now they had the power of the military on theirs. It would hardly be surprising if, in these circumstances, Michael felt the need to be in the company of friends rather than alone in his house. His close friends from the *MAPU* Action Group were unsuitable: their homes were likely to be searched and his presence might compromise them. At all events, late that afternoon or early in the evening he arrived at the Martínez home together with a working man from his district.[4] A total curfew had been announced by the military authorities but at this stage it was still incompletely enforced. He and Javier moved into the house of a neighbour and stayed there for a while. But this neighbour was a former Communist and his house was likely to be searched, so they returned to the Martínez house where they both spent the night. Michael slept in Javier's room. Javier slept in his brother's.

Early next morning, Wednesday, 12th, Michael decided it would be safer to go to a house in Recreo, a hillside district of Viña to the north of Placeres, belonging to a school friend of Isabel called Georgina Becerra. Javier's girl friend, Bárbara, arrived at the Martínez house just as Michael and Javier were setting out, so she accompanied them to Recreo. To avoid patrols and road blocks, they made their way on foot across the intervening hills and gullies. When they reached the house, Bárbara and Javier stayed a short time, then left Michael there. Georgina was at home with her three younger children. Her husband was away during the week, working on the railways, and her eldest son was also absent, so Michael was able to sleep in his bed in the boys' room.[5]

The following morning, Thursday,13th September, Javier and Bárbara returned to the house in Recreo. They were surprised to find Michael sitting on a chair calmly reading a Physics book. He was considering how to get to Santiago, he told them, for he believed the workers there were better organised and resistance to the Coup would be more effective than it had been in Valparaiso. He gave Javier and Bárbara some messages for members of the Action Group and other friends in Placeres.[6]

In fact Michael stayed with Georgina and her children for nine days, until Friday, 21st. There was a good collection of books in the house and he spent the time reading and praying, cleaning the house for the family and washing clothes. According to his hostess, he felt very strongly the injustice of the situation but was calm and grateful. Before the family meals he said Grace. For Georgina it was a worrying time. Her husband was away. She had her children and a political refugee to look after. The schools were closed, as they would have been anyway, until the 20th, the day after the Independence Day celebrations. 'We heard military vehicles coming to neighbouring houses and expected them at any moment to knock on our door'. When Georgina's husband returned from work at the week-end there was a certain awkwardness because he fully supported the military Regime. Conversation at meals was confined to small talk.[7]

Friday, 14th September, was to have been the day of Michael's stag night party. He had planned to hold it at his own house that evening. The civil marriage was to take place the next day in a registry office near Isabel's home. On Tuesday,18th, to coincide with the national holiday, there was to be an informal ceremony and party with all their friends at Michael's house. Although the curfew was lifted between 8am and 7pm from the 14th onwards, it was forbidden to gather in groups. So parties were out of the question. The previous Sunday, 9th September, Michael had confided to a friend[8] a presentiment that his marriage would not take place. By the morning of the 14th, if not earlier, it was clear that the presentiment was accurate, for the time being at least. Either on Thursday 13th or Friday 14th Georgina took a letter from Michael to Isabel in Quillota warning her that he could not risk travelling for the civil wedding ceremony on the Saturday.

Pepo Gutiérrez recalls Michael coming to his mother's house in Viña, where he also lived, a few days after the Coup, around midday.[9] His mother gave them coffee. Michael needed to discuss the postponement of his wedding arrangements with Pepo who was to have played an important part in them. He was to have attended the wedding in Michael's house on 18th September. It had been planned as a social event with friends present so that they would all know that he and Isabel were married, with a prayer and blessing given by Pepo, but not a sacramental or canonical marriage.[10]

Michael stayed with Pepo for twenty minutes. Pepo invited him to move into his mother's house for a time — she was very fond of him. Michael declined, saying that he had no reason to hide; he had done nothing wrong. He had only been trying to live out the demands of the Gospel. Pepo remembers making a black joke which turned out to be grimly prophetic: 'Remember that as a Gringo you are wired for 115 volts', Pepo said. 'In Chile it's 220 volts, so get yourself fitted with a transformer'. Even educated South Americans are liable to regard Englishmen as Yankees.[11]

Michael also visited Myrta Crocco sometime during his nine days in Recreo. He arrived at her house in Viña in the late afternoon and spent two and a half hours there.[12] He appeared calm but was very concerned about the fate of fellow political activists. He knew that people had been beaten up. 'We were all dejected and so was he', Myrta remembered. He told her that he was required to report to Naval Headquarters in the port in Valparaiso and wasn't sure what he should do. 'We felt confused, especially us older ones, taken by surprise. This had never happened in Chile. Usually Michael was so clear and decisive. His uncertainty was a sign of how confused we all were. He needed to think things out. We didn't know what was happening. I was surprised that he was on the wanted list. He didn't know why. He said he had nothing to hide. Everyone knew how he lived — in Cerro Placeres, at the University, in Calera. His life was an open book'. Myrta assured him that in the circumstances it was healthy and normal to be unsure what action to take. He repeated that he had absolutely nothing to hide and then seemed to come to a decision: he would go to Naval Headquarters the next day. He then told Myrta about his wedding arrangements for the 18th and his doubt as to whether it would take place. This came as a complete surprise to her: until then she had no idea of his intention to marry. She had never heard Isabel mentioned before and was not sure if even at this stage Michael told her her name. If he did so, she forgot it. Myrta had been accustomed to a more or less professional relationship with Michael: they were University colleagues with similar political sympathies and commitments. This reference to his personal life was uncharacteristic and particularly moving for that reason. His words about the marriage were spoken wistfully. Myrta told him there was no need to put it off. It was always good to share a party, even under the present circumstances.[13]

He stayed late. The house was 'like a beehive'. In addition to Myrta's six children there was a mother and her daughter, the wife of a friend who had been taken away by the Military. Michael and Myrta talked in her bedroom. He sat on the bed. She was on a stool beside him. Afterwards he stayed with her children and Myrta served tea. Someone else arrived from the Cerro. Someone came to tell a local schoolboy who was visiting not to go home because the Military were looking for him. Myrta asked Michael to come back after he had been to Naval Headquarters and let her know how it went. He said he would come back the next day.[14]

Sometime during the first days after the Coup Michael's house was searched. A neighbour of his[15] met a local shopkeeper[16] in the road nearby. He was a person with whom Michael, as President of the Provision and Price Committee, had had some strong disagreements. The shopkeeper asked the way to Michael's house. Without thinking, the neighbour indicated the direction. The shopkeeper was followed at a short distance, by a detachment of Marines. They surrounded the house, aiming their guns at it, then forced their way in, breaking down the door and smashing a window. [17]

The house contained some compromising material: Jaime Contreras, the last of the students who had stayed with Michael, was a Philosophy Research Assistant at the Catholic University. He too was in the process of moving out before the wedding planned for the 18th, and was not there at the time of the Coup. His particular interest was Karl Marx. He was writing a thesis on the implicit theory of knowledge in *Das Kapital*. His books, packed in boxes awaiting removal to his mother's house in Viña, were mostly of a kind likely to confirm the suspicions of the Military.[18] According to neighbours, the Marines drove off with several jeep loads of books and documents, presumably including Jaime's boxes. Not having found Michael at home, Naval patrols regularly went back to the house looking for him. He himself learned of this and of the break in and search while he was hiding in Recreo.

On Friday, 21st September,[19] the Rector of the Catholic University,[20] called a meeting of academic staff at eleven o'clock in the morning. That morning Javier Martínez and Bárbara planned to visit Michael and tell him about the meeting. But at 9am, before they had set out, Michael appeared on their doorstep. Javier asked him whether it was wise to risk being seen out and about on Cerro Placeres. Michael said he had nothing to fear. It was possible that friends from the Action Group had visited him in Recreo and, seeing that they moved about without hindrance, he felt able to do the same.[21] But if, as Javier believed, Michael knew that his house had been searched, it seems strange that he should be so sanguine. Perhaps his indignation at the injustice of the Coup, coupled with a characteristic streak of obstinacy and the knowledge that he had always acted with integrity under the law, gradually overcame fears of reprisal and punishment.

At all events Javier and Michael set off together, catching a bus from Placeres into the City. The meeting took place in the Engineering building. The Rector had called it in order to inform the Staff that his own post and the whole University were being taken over by the Navy. The meeting lasted an hour. When it ended Javier left and Michael remained with some of his *CESCLA* colleagues who had also been present,[22] The Secretary of *CESCLA*, Georgina Arangua, and Michael went off to lunch in a nearby restaurant. They ate their meal in a secluded compartment. In their conversation they shared their uncertainty as to what they should do and as to how the Naval authorities would act. They knew that people were being arrested and detained; they did not know that some were dying. There had been no massacres under the Naval regime in Valparaiso as there had been under the Army rule in Santiago. Georgina's opinion was that if they are going to catch up with you eventually, the sooner it happens the better. Then the matter can be laid to rest. He had nothing to hide. Michael was very quiet and listened attentively. Georgina thought he was in agreement. They finished the meal and had parted by 2pm.[23]

The probability is that at this point Michael returned to Viña. He may have paid his visit to Myrta later that afternoon,[24] returned to the Becerras' house to collect his belongings and eventually, but before the 8pm curfew, made his way back to Placeres. Manuel takes up the story and recounts their disagreement:

He came to our house in the evening. We were amazed because we knew they were on the look-out for him. There were many informers around so Delfina and I had not been to Michael's house during his absence. He ate a meal with us. He said he was fed up with hiding and saw no reason to continue doing so. I was Secretary of a Land Occupation Committee and a Provision and Price Committee officer and I was able to walk around publicly. So why couldn't he do the same? I pointed out that the tradesmen had a grudge against him, but not against me since there weren't any in my district. He was keen to go and see what state his house was in and determined to spend the night there. We reminded him that a number of his neighbours were political opponents and that people had been to his house looking for him. But he would not be persuaded.[25]

Later that same night Michael went back to Poblacion Progreso and with the help of a neighbour[26] secured the doors and windows which the Marines had smashed open. At half past midnight, evidently flouting the curfew, he appeared at the house of another neighbour, his friend Luis Rodríguez, 'looking angry and dejected'. From there he returned to his own house.[27]

Informers must indeed have been on the look-out for him. There was a retired member of the Navy living across the road in Buenos Aires Street. It may have been he who, seeing a light in Michael's house, telephoned Naval Intelligence to let them know Michael was back. In the early hours, allegedly witnessed by the neighbour across the road who used to provide meals for Michael and the students when they lived together, a jeep came and took him away when everybody was asleep.[28]

It is not certain where Michael was taken. His arrest would have been ordered by Naval Intelligence but could have been carried out by the Police, in which case he would have been taken initially to the nearest Police Station[29] and then handed over to the Marines — the

Navy's land forces. It is more likely that he was arrested by the Marines and taken either to the Naval Training School (*Academia de Guerra*) where many prisoners were held and interrogated at this time or, more probably, to one of the two prison ships moored in Valparaiso harbour. What is certain is that he ended up on board one of them.

The two ships were the *Lebu*, a merchant vessel belonging to the Pacific Navigation Company, which had had a fire in the engine room. While it was awaiting repairs its owners offered it to the *Junta* for use as a prison ship. Within a few days of the Coup a thousand prisoners were squashed into its hold which had no sanitary facilities and no proper feeding arrangements. Both feeding and slopping out were done by letting down buckets from the quay a couple of times a day. The other vessel was the training ship and pride of the Chilean Navy, *La Esmeralda*, affectionately known as *La Dama Blanca* — the White Lady. She is a tall ship with four masts and an auxiliary engine. Below decks were two compartments each with bunks for forty to fifty midshipmen. Each year the newly graduated Midshipmen sail *La Esmeralda* around the world calling in at friendly ports. Most Chilean Naval Officers have proud memories of the world tour when it was their turn to form the Crew, and are ashamed of, and even deny, the fact that *La Dama Blanca* was used as a place of interrogation and torture of political prisoners after the Coup.

According to the dating I have put forward, Michael was arrested in the early hours Saturday, 22nd September, 1973, was interrogated, and died six or seven hours later as a result of the treatment he received at the hands of his interrogators. This very tight timing is perfectly possible and I have based it on the evidence of Georgina Becerra who states categorically that Michael was in her house for nine days from the 12th, and of Georgina Arangua, Secretary of *CESCLA*, who had lunch with Michael after the meeting at the University which she calculates took place on the 21st. These are both first-hand witnesses and people whose judgment is trustworthy. There exists, however, a body of opinion which is not in agreement with this dating, though it does not conflict with the facts.

On the morning of Thursday, 20th September, a lady[30] who lived in Recreo, Viña del Mar, received a phone call from a neighbour telling her that her husband, an elderly medical doctor who had been detained by the Military, was free. He was in fact in the street at the bottom of the hill leading to their house in a state of collapse. When they got him home and he regained full consciousness all he could talk about was Michael Woodward. He and Michael had been together on the *Esmeralda*. At one point the Doctor, with his medical knowledge, recognised that Michael had gone into a state of auricular fibrillation and told the guard that he would die unless he received proper attention immediately.[31] The guard replied that, as far as he was concerned, he could die. Shortly after this there was a change of guards and the new guards called for medical help.

Another witness[32] who was detained on the *Lebu* states that Michael, whom he had not previously known, arrived on board the *Lebu* on Sunday,16th or Monday,17th. He was dazed and in a poor way. But he was one of the 'specials' who were removed to the *Esmeralda* and did not return to the *Lebu*. 'Specials' were prisoners considered to be important, high ranking officials of the Allende Regime or of local government, and the like. There does not seem to have been any special delicacy in their treatment.

A Socialist City Councillor of Valparaiso, also detained on the *Esmeralda*, claims that, although he did not see Michael himself, he was told by a crew member a day or two before he left for exile on Dawson Island on the 20th, that there was a priest on board, presumably in the other compartment.[33]

Myrta Crocco places Michael's visit to her earlier than the 21st. She recalls that a couple of days after Michael left her, saying he would go and present himself at Naval Headquarters, his fiancée, Isabel, appeared at her house with blankets because she believed that Michael was in prison. Myrta took the blankets the next day to Valparaiso. In one of the banks in the city centre was a long queue, stretching out into the street, of people with blankets for prisoners on board the *Lebu*. She thought Michael must be on the *Lebu* since that, apparently, was where all those people who had not returned home were being held prisoner. She joined the queue with a blanket with Michael's name on it. A sailor asked her what her relationship with him was. She said she was a friend but knew that he would assume that Michael was her lover, so she deposited the blanket on a large table and left without giving her name. Later Isabel phoned to ask if Myrta had got the blankets to Michael. Myrta told her what she had done, but added that she had seen no list with Michael's name on it.[34]

Though there is disagreement about the timing, it is certain that Michael was detained on board the *Esmeralda*. This certainty derives, not principally from the convergent testimony of these witnesses, but from an unguarded report in the Valparaiso evening paper *La Estrella*, based on an official briefing, which mentions the *Esmeralda* as the place where he was being held prisoner. In recent years and in response to protests at foreign ports it has visited, the Chilean Navy claim that the *Esmeralda* was not used as a prison ship after the Coup. At the time, journalists of *La Estrella* were informed otherwise. They had no reason to invent it. The report will be quoted in full later, when other matters arising from its contents are considered.

It is also certain that in the course of his interrogation

Michael was tortured.[35] The *Lebu* and *Esmeralda* were not the only vessels moored alongside the jetty in Valparaiso harbour. The *Lebu* was at the seaward end and the *Esmeralda* at the end nearest the shore. In between them lay the Chilean naval cruiser *Latorre* with a crew of a thousand. They had been in these positions since before the Coup. When the rest of the fleet left port on the 10th September, pretending to join the United States naval force at sea, the *Latorre* remained in the harbour, ostensibly to undergo repairs but in reality because it was to serve as a fully equipped communications centre for the Coup. All three vessels were still in the same positions alongside the jetty a couple of weeks later.[36]

One morning, about ten days after the Coup, the Commander of the *Latorre*, Captain Carlos Fanta, was in his wardroom at about seven o'clock when an urgent request arrived from the *Esmeralda* for a doctor to attend a prisoner who was critically ill. Since Admiral Merino, the Naval Commander-in-Chief, was away in Santiago attending a meeting of the *Junta*, Fanta was the senior officer in the port that day. He was concerned about conditions on the Lebu, to which he sent food from the *Latorre's* galley, and about possible abuse of prisoners. So he not only sent one of the two doctors in his crew to the *Esmeralda*, but ordered him to report back immediately on his return to the *Latorre*.[37]

The Doctor returned at about eight o'clock. The table in the wardroom was laid for breakfast. He told the Captain that the prisoner, a priest from Cerro Placeres, was suffering from serious internal injuries, his internal organs were ruptured and haemorrhaging. He could not live for more than another hour at the most. Dr Gleiser had ordered him to be taken to the Naval Hospital. He told Fanta that the injuries were undoubtedly caused by severe blows to the body.[38]

Chilean Marines were trained to punch those who

143

were undergoing interrogation when the answers to questions were not forthcoming or were considered unsatisfactory. After the Coup they adopted the American method of wrapping their fists in wet towels which would prevent their punches from leaving marks on the victim's body. Michael, being exceptionally tall and thin, was especially vulnerable to this treatment and his internal organs correspondingly less protected.

The Naval Hospital was not far but there would have been a delay while they waited for an ambulance. As Michael lay on the deck of the *Esmeralda*, or on the quay nearby, bleeding to death, he experienced in different circumstances the ultimate persecution for justice's sake undergone by the Old Testament prophets on whom he had frequently meditated. He relived in his own particular way the sufferings of Christ at the hands of powerful men. Though in a different manner from what he had anticipated, his role as priest was now accomplished by the shedding of blood. Some unsubstantiated evidence indicates that he did not reach the hospital alive but died in the ambulance on the way.[39]

The death certificate states that Michael died of 'cardio-respiratory arrest'.[40] The place of death is said to have been the public highway (*via publica*) in Valparaiso, the time 12 noon on Saturday, 22nd September. Death 'on the public highway' was an expression sometimes used to indicate or insinuate that the person had been killed in armed combat. This allegation was made against Michael and has persisted to the present.[41] The more obvious interpretation is that he died in the ambulance before reaching the hospital.

The story is now taken up by the Chaplain to the Naval Hospital, Eduardo Stangher Abel.[42] On the morning of Saturday, 22nd September the Chaplain went into the Hospital as usual between eight and half-past. On arriving he was told that there was a '*padrecito*' in the morgue. He went immediately to see who it was. The body was on a table, covered with a sheet which Stangher lifted. He recognised Michael Woodward. He then gave him the Last Sacraments conditionally, anointing his forehead, nose, eyes, ears and hands. His face appeared 'normal'. After visiting the sick in the hospital he went to inform the diocesan authorities. He thought he went personally but was not sure whom he spoke to. He told them the situation and said that it was up to them to do something about it. The authorities told Stangher that Michael was not their responsibility since he no longer belonged to the diocesan clergy. This was news to him since he had not heard of Michael's suspension the year before. The Bishop was away. At our first interview Stangher said that no one in the diocesan offices wished to get involved and, since Michael had no relatives in the country, the Naval authorities undertook the burial themselves.

The aftermath of Michael's death was remembered differently by the man who at that time was Vicar General of the Diocese, Monsignor Jorge Bosagna. According to his version, Stangher telephoned him at home to let him know that he had just administered the Last Sacraments to Michael Woodward who was either *in articulo mortis* or had just died. It was a Saturday. Stangher said Michael Woodward had died from a heart attack and asked Bosagna what he should do since he considered it was the Vicar General's responsibility to decide. Bosagna told Stangher he would inform the Bishop, added that Michael had no relatives in Chile and that it was a complex matter because he was not a member of the clergy either. He had abandoned the ministry *de facto*. Bosagna said that he didn't know of any appropriate legal procedure. He told Stangher that nevertheless the diocese would take charge of his burial and that he would instruct an undertaker.

Sunday was a difficult day, but on Monday, Bosagna

remembered telling Stangher, he would offer a Mass for Michael in private and arrange for the burial in the vault reserved for the Valparaiso clergy in the Cemetery of Playa Ancha. Stangher pointed out that this would require the permission of the Naval authorities. So they agreed to meet at four or four-thirty in the afternoon with the Commander-in-Chief at Naval Headquarters. They went there, Bosagna continued, and waited but were unable to have an interview because the Admiral was absent. Bosagna then instructed the undertaker, since it was late on Saturday, to wait until the body was handed over to them, probably on Monday. The next day, Sunday, the Chaplain telephoned Bosagna again to say that he had been informed that the Naval authorities would take care of the burial themselves. Bosagna then told the undertaker that they would not need his services and informed the Bishop of what had happened.[43]

Confronted with Mgr Bosagna's evidence, Fr Stangher modified his version only slightly: he informed the diocesan authorities and, having done that, judged that his responsibility was at an end. The authorities told him of Michael's suspension from the priesthood and said they would consider what to do. Stangher stated that he would have gone personally on such a matter, not telephoned and he had no recollection of going for a meeting at Naval Headquarters.

The point at issue in this divergence of memories is whether the Naval authorities withheld the body to prevent it being examined or whether they buried it themselves because the Church authorities washed their hands of any responsibility in the matter. The warm support shown by Bishop Tagle for the new military *Junta* doubtless pervaded the Diocesan Curia and it seems likely that the Church leadership in Valparaiso wished to distance itself from left wing priests, such as Michael, who were an embarrassment to it. Chaplain Stangher's statement that

146

'no one in the diocesan offices wished to get involved' is probably accurate.[44]

Whatever the conflicting memories as to who took or did not take responsibility for Michael's body, there is agreement that his burial was arranged by the Navy, and arranged at no cost to itself: he was placed in the paupers' grave, a large pit at the edge of the Cemetery of Playa Ancha in which unclaimed bodies were placed without individual identification.[45]

It was on the very day on which his death certificate states that he died, Saturday 22nd September, that the report of Michael's arrest and detention appeared in the Valparaiso evening paper *La Estrella*:

> In an operation undertaken last night in the sector of Cerro Los Placeres Naval personnel arrested an ex-priest named Michael Woodward Irribarren (*sic*) of 30 years of age. In his possession were found much extremist propaganda, plans for a combat operation on the 17th (September) and (details of) some breaches of trust, relating to his work in the confessional as a priest, with under-age girls. The personnel who took part in the operation, after a short interrogation, left him on board the *Esmeralda* where at this moment he remains in custody. Up to this point we know that the pseudo-priest took part in various attacks on police in the Province of Valparaiso and, according to a notebook found in his possession, he had sexually abused an indeterminate number of young girls.

This report is in the form of an official press briefing by the Naval authorities given on the morning of 22nd September. Though the briefing does not mention his death, the Naval authorities who authorised it must have known that Michael had already died. They were making use of preemptive character assassination to spike any possible protest by the Church or others. The misspelling of his maternal name Irriberry may have been a misprint.

It may, on the other hand, have been deliberate since the family (of his grandmother) was known and respected in Viña. The inaccuracy over his age — he was forty-one, not thirty — again may have been deliberate: perhaps thirty was considered a more plausible age for one who engaged in both armed attacks on the police and seduction of under-age girls.

Allegations of armed resistance and sexual irresponsibility reveal the character of the military imagination. The first is incompatible with what is known of Michael's movements after the Coup. For the second there is no evidence. The alleged notebook has not been produced. The Chilean Navy must now be embarrassed by their own briefing concerning the *Esmeralda*. The statement that Michael was arrested 'last night' and the reference to a 'short interrogation' are further evidence for my version of the timing of Michael's final days.

Sadly, the attempt to discredit Michael and others who suffered a similar fate succeeded with those who supported the Coup. They were so relieved at the restoration of order after the chaos of recent months and years that they were prepared to believe whatever the military authorities told them. Myrta Crocco had a chance encounter with a senior diocesan priest some days later:

> One day, having gone to the Catholic University, I bumped into Father (Monsignor) Jorge Sapunar. He told me he had been present at a Mass for a priest in the diocesan offices. It was a private Mass celebrated for Michael Woodward who had died, he said, on the *Lebu* (*sic*). Sapunar added how good it was of the Bishop to say the Mass because all that Michael had been up to had appeared in the newspaper.

Myrta got hold of the relevant edition of *La Estrella* and went to find Sapunar. 'This isn't Michael', she said. He replied: 'Myrta, we are all confused. When the Navy took control of Valparaiso, I drank champagne in the street with my next-door neighbours'.[46]

So Bishop Emilio Tagle finally celebrated a Requiem Mass for Michael, asking God to be merciful in his judgment. It may not have occurred to him that Michael's death placed him also under judgment. In the Bishop's view Michael was misguided and his death was the unfortunate consequence of his errors. How different it would have been if the former Seminary Rector and student had been able to speak, trust and listen to each other. Don Emilio's belief that Communism was the greatest enemy led to his uncritical support of the Pinochet Regime, lending it a respectability which, for his fellow-bishops, it increasingly forfeited. Michael's conviction that the poverty and insecurity of the people he lived among in the *poblaciones* were an injustice crying out to Heaven and were caused by the blindness and selfishness of the rich led him along a lonely path to torture and death. That he did not betray his friends and fellow activists by giving away their names under torture, as they testify,[47] that they remember him with such affection that they named their sons after him, confirms what is revealed by the whole of his life: he was a man of straightforward, but obstinate, integrity who single-mindedly strove to live, work and, when it was necessary, die as a disciple of his Lord. But what he saw as the Lord's work he carried out in a secular, political environment, by secular and political means. In that world, largely alienated from God and from religious practice, he was a gentle and powerful witness. In the words of a friend and fellow *poblacion* dweller: 'In Michael Woodward they killed a man who wouldn't harm a fly. He never offended anyone: never an insult or coarse word. He had charisma and got on well with ordinary people: so they believed he was a dangerous leader. He never did anything violent'.[48]

1. Javier was Michael's assistant and taught physics in *CESCLA*.
2. Manuel Rojas 1990.
3. Eduardo Catalan 1990.
4. Javier Martínez 1992.
5. Georgina Becerra 1996.
6. Javier and Bárbara Martínez 1992.
7. Georgina Becerra 1996.
8. Carmen Rojas de G. 1990.
9. Pepo Gutiérrez 1990.
10. The Bishop may have got wind of Michael's intention because at about this time Pepo received a circular letter from his office forbidding the presence or participation of priests at the weddings of 'consecrated persons not in possession of a dispensation from their vows'. Although he was not mentioned by name, Michael was the only such person in the Diocese of Valparaiso at the time the circular was sent.
11. Pepo was a skilled electrician and earned his living by this for fourteen years when he became estranged from the diocese after being himself interrogated and tortured a few weeks later with what he believed to be the connivance of the Church authorities. (Pepo Gutiérrez 1990).
12. Myrta Crocco 1990.
13. ibid.
14. ibid. If the chronology in this chapter is correct Michael did not go to Valparaiso the next day. If he did so, then Myrta's dating is wrong.
15. Orlando Malladares.
16. Francisco Raggio.
17. Orlando Malladares.
18. Jaime Contreras.
19. According to Georgina Arangua, Secretary to *CESCLA*, the meeting took place ten days after the coup.
20. Raúl Allard.
21. This is what Javier Martínez surmised.
22. Javier Martínez 1992. It was the last time they saw each other.
23. Georgina Arangua 1996.
24. If the schoolboy mentioned by Myrta was actually on his way home from school, as Myrta implied, this would make sense since schools only reopened on Thursday, 20th.
25. Manuel Rojas 1990.
26. Orlando Malladares 1990.
27. Luis Rodríguez 1990.
28. This neighbour's evidence was recalled by Manuel Rojas in 1990, but not confirmed.
29. On *Cerro Baron*.
30. I interviewed Alicia Gil de Zamorano in 1992. Her husband had died

many years before. He had been a medical doctor in Vina and a member of the Communist Party of Chile, considerably older than her and suffering at the time of the Coup from severe diabetes. He had officially retired from medical practice but continued working when other doctors withheld their services during the later months of Allende's Government. According to his widow's recollection, Dr Zamorano was arrested at his house on the night of the 12th-13th September. The Marines came at 11.30pm, searched the house for over two hours, then took Dr Zamorano away at around 2am to the Naval Training School (*Academia de Guerra*) where he was interrogated during the rest of the night being given electric shocks and placed in a freezing bath. At 7am he was taken away and placed on board the *Esmeralda* where the interrogation with electric shocks continued. They were applied to his temples, chest, genitals and fingers. His body was wet and the shocks caused him to jump in the air. The house search and the interrogation were based on the assumption that arms for the uprising were hidden and that a secret hospital was being set up to treat the wounded.

31. Auricular fibrilation occurs when one part of the heart beats at a very fast rate while the other part beats slowly. This brings about a potentially fatal lack of oxygen in the blood. The condition can be caused by certain types of electric shock.

32. Jorge Gabaude 1990.

33. Maximiliano Marholz 1992.

34 Myrta Crocco 1990. This recollection presents more problems since Michael's arrest and detention were announced (after he had, in fact died) in the Valparaiso evening paper, *La Estrella*, on 22nd September.

35. Two *Esmeralda* prisoners to whom I spoke in 1992 described their experience on board as folllows: Maximiliano Marholz, a former medical orderly and instructor who had served for 25 years in the Chilean Navy, was arrested in the late evening of the 11th and detained on the *Esmeralda* from then until the 20th when he was flown to Dawson Island. He was made to strip to his underpants on arrival, forced to the ground, face down and trampled on. He was then removed to a different part of the ship to be interrogated and tortured. The questions always concerned the supposed hiding-places of weapons.

Sergio Vuskovic, a professor of philosophy, member of the Communist Party and Mayor of Valparaiso was also held on the *Esmeralda*, at first in the Chaplain's cabin and later in the infirmary. In the infirmary he was interrogated and tortured. Naked and tied to a chair he was punched and kicked all over apart from his face and had electric current applied to all parts of his body, especially his genitals, fingers and teeth. He was hosed with icy water. The interrogation and torture according to Vuskovic was undertaken by Naval officers. Prisoners were kicked and punched in the infirmary but the water and electric shock torture was apparently applied on deck. Vuskovic did not see or know

Michael on the *Esmeralda*.

36. This and the subsequent testimony is given by Captain Carlos Fanta. I was put in touch with the retired naval Captain,Carlos Fanta, by a senior priest of the Diocese of Valparaiso who for many years has led a weekly prayer or Bible study group of which Fanta was a member. The evidence which he gave me and which he subsequently submitted to the Commission for Justice and Truth (*Comision Rettig*) set up by President Aylwin in 1990 had been consistently made available to the members of the prayer group and to other friends over many years and had never been treated as a secret.

Carlos Fanta had commanded the *Esmeralda* on its world cruise in 1968 and, by virtue of this fact, many middle-ranking naval officers had served under him. Senior officers including those who organised the Coup were his colleagues. At the time of the Coup he was the senior captain in the Chilean navy, due at any moment to be promoted Admiral. He supported the Coup's aims, but on the understanding that elections would be called within sixty days. His opinion was that the members of the military *Junta*, all of whom he knew personally, enjoyed the experience of power so much that they were unwilling to relinquish it.

In October,1973, the *Latorre*, which Fanta commanded, was due for a refit and Fanta was ordered to Talcahuano, in the south, as temporary commander of one of the military zones into which the country was divided during the state of siege. Part of his work involved presiding at the tribunals which tried all those political activists of the Left (including Government ministers) who had supported a transition to Socialism under Allende. Many of these were condemned to death. Fanta, however, stepped out of line with his colleagues by refusing to pass the death sentence on anyone brought before him. As a result of this, he claimed, he received on the 29th October an order to retire from the Service. He was not further harassed and found a job for the next fifteen years piloting merchant vessels between Buenos Aires and the ports of Chile via the Magellan Straits. Although the facts he told me about his career might have given him cause for resentment against the Pinochet regime, I gained the impression of a man of integrity who had sufficient moral weight among his former colleagues to speak his mind openly.

37. Doctor Kenneth Gleiser Joo.

38. Fanta told me this story on the 18th August 1990. On the 11th September, after he had attempted to get his story confirmed by Dr Gleiser he informed me that Gleiser, who was then still a serving officer in the Navy, declined to meet Fanta for a conversation and declared that he did not remember any of this: 'There were so many cases of the kind'. Fanta, in correcting his own story, later told me that on consulting colleagues he now believed that Michael had not been detained on the *Esmeralda* at all but had been brought there, presumably from the *Lebu*, in a critical state, quite unable to walk and had been attended by Dr

Gleiser either on the quay or on the deck of the *Esmeralda*. Much as I respected Captain Fanta's integrity, I tend to doubt this correction in view of the strong feelings which Fanta and other officers had for the *Esmeralda*, the evidence of Alicia Gil de Zamorano, Jorge Gabaude and Maximiliano Marholz and, most especially, the unwitting evidence of the Valparaiso evening paper *La Estrella* for the 22nd September, a paper which had to pass military censorship. The Captain of the *Esmeralda* at this time was Captain (later Admiral) Jorge Sabugo Silva.

39. In his later years in the Navy, Councillor Marholz had been an instructor of medical orderlies in the Naval Medical School in Valparaiso. In a conversation with me in 1992, he claimed to have met by chance one of his former students who told him that he had attended the Gringo priest in the ambulance and that he died on the way to the hospital. Marholz could not remember the student's name. In view of its coincidence with but independence from the evidence of Carlos Fanta, this seems likely to be true.

40. *Paro cardio-respiratorio* caused by *T.E.C. agudo cerrado*. It was signed by Dr Costa Canessa.

41. In September 1992 the Senior Chaplain to the Chilean Navy, Fr Gustavo Adolfo Garcia, assured me in an angry telephone conversation that Michael had died leading a band of terrorists in a street shoot-out. Fr Garcia had preached a sermon the day before at the Naval parade marking the nineteenth anniversary of the Coup.

42. Fr Eduardo Stangher Abel was a priest of the Diocese of Valparaiso who had been seconded to the Navy Vicariate. He had known Michael both at seminary and at the chaplains' house in Valparaiso where they had both lived between 1964 and 1966. Stangher had been Chaplain of the Naval Hospital in Valparaiso since the beginning of 1973.

43. Mgr Jorge Bosagna 1990.

44. At the time they spoke to me Stangher was retired from the Navy, receiving a substantial naval pension and living in an apartment block owned (and guarded) by the Navy. Bosagna was still doing some work at the diocesan offices and lecturing on Moral Theology and Ethics at the Catholic University. Each had a motive to defend his respective institution. Stangher was nervous and guarded in what he said. Bosagna was smooth and loquacious. I tended at first to discount Stangher's claim that on entering the morgue at the Naval Hospital he took the sheet right off Michael's body to see if there were wounds or marks and there were none. If he indeed did what he said, it indicated his suspicions as to the cause of Michael's death. When I later confronted him with the evidence of Captain Carlos Fanta his reply was: 'It's the same as you (British) did in Northern Ireland'.

45. The register at the Cemetery of Playa Ancha contains an entry for Tuesday, 25th September 1973 to the effect that Michael Woodward had on that day been buried in the common grave (*fosa comun*). A workman

at the Cemetery showed me the way to where, in 1973, the common grave would have been. The gate in the Cemetery wall which used to lead out to it had, in recent years, been walled up and over the spot where the grave had been, now outside the Cemetery, there was a new road, the *Avenida Costanera*. The road is a few yards from the cliff edge, overlooking the Pacific Ocean.

46. There were other examples of the press collaborating with the new Regime in blackening the reputation of a left wing priest. At the presbytery in La Aurora, Vina del Mar, where two Dutch priests were arrested, they 'found injections of sexual stimulants'. It was the new Regime's way of justifying its actions.

47. Eduardo Catalan 1992.

48. Nano Rojas 1996.

BIBLIOGRAPHY

Leslie Bethell (ed): *Chile since Independence*
(Cambridge University Press, 1993).

Diocese of Valparaiso Archives.

Downside School Archives.

Nathaniel Davis: *The Last Two Years of Salvador Allende*
(Cornell University, 1985).

Brian Loveman: *Chile — The Legacy of Spanish Capitalism*
(Oxford University Press, 1979. 2nd ed.1988).

Pablo Richard: *Cristianos por el Socialismo*
Historia y Documentacion
(Ediciones Sigueme, Salamanca, 1976).

Brian H.Smith: *The Church and Politics in Chile*
Challenges to Modern Catholicism
(Princeton University Press, 1983).

David O.Toledo: *Monsenor Emilio Tagle, Vigia de la Fe*
(Editorial Senda, Valparaiso, 1988).

Arturo Valenzuela: 'Chile'
[series *The Breakdown of Democratic Regimes*]
(Johns Hopkins University Press, 1978).